SACRED *freedom*

WESTERN LIBERALIST IDEOLOGIES IN THE LIGHT OF ISLAM

*H*aneef *O*liver

ISBN: 0-9776996-0-9

Library of Congress Control Number: 2005938193

Cover Design: *Asl Concept and Design* (aslconcept@earthlink.net)
Published in the United States by WestPoint Publishing.
Distributed to the trade by BookMasters.
2541 Ashland Road
Mansfield, OH 44905

Available online and in bookstores.
For quantity orders and discounts, call: 800-247-6553 (Fax: 419-281-6883)
Email: orders@bookmasters.com

Setting our own bounds of freedom appears to be liberating and attractive like the limitless nature of a gleaming, bright sky. However, what really lies behind this image that we create for ourselves?

Contents

Introduction

After the events of September 11, I saw the need to compile a book about terrorism and religious extremism in the world today. After publishing this book, it occurred to me that another subject - that of negligence in religious affairs - was also in desperate need of being addressed for both Muslim and non-Muslim readers.

On a daily basis, we are being inundated with different kinds of man-made liberalist ideologies in the mainstream media. Because of the sheer volume and almost monotone voice of many media outlets, people are given the impression that these ideologies must be accepted by every living individual and society in the world today, and that the validity of these ideologies is not open to question.

At present, Westerners and liberalists in general are intrigued as to why people are still turning to Islaam for enlightenment in this modern age. This is particularly intriguing for those who are convinced that Islaam is something that impedes progress, and that Islaamic civilization has proven to be inferior to other civilizations as a result of its adherence to Islaam. This subject has been addressed in this book as a response to Italian Prime Minister Silvio Berlusconi's remark that Islaamic civilization is "stuck where it was 1400 years ago."[1]

I have also analyzed the two main reference points in Western humanist thinking throughout the book. The first of these is the belief that people are free and responsible for deciding their own actions, and therefore, that God should only have a personal, marginal place in their lives. The other important point of reference for Western policy and societal orientation is the belief that the opinion of the majority should act as mankind's principle criterion in shaping human behaviour and legislation.

---

[1] Berlusconi: The West must conquer Islam, *Associated Press: Salon*, September 26, 2001.

One of the major points of contention that liberalists have with Islaam is the reluctance the Muslim world has shown in embracing these two principles. Some liberalists take a more militant approach in trying to spread these two principles in the Muslim world, while others censure these tactics, hoping that more temperate policies will win the Muslims over to contemporary humanist values. Whatever the method, the message remains the same: Muslims must change their beliefs and eventually conform to this ever-changing series of humanist values.

After reading this book, the reader will be able to judge whether the devotion that people have towards these two principles is deserved, and whether there is any basis for people's opposition to the principles of Islaam.

The reader will notice that the first two chapters establish certain essential matters that are referred to later on when discussing issues related to contemporary Western ideologies. The first chapter deals with the subject of how we can know that a Creator does actually exist, while the second chapter deals with why this Creator deserves to be worshipped and served alone in our lives.

It should be noted that the concept of worship in Islaam is much broader than just a limited set of religious rites. Prayer, charity, good treatment of parents, decency towards people and excellence in the workplace are only a few examples of how a Muslim is expected to worship the Creator.

In order to substantiate what I have written from an Islaamic perspective, I have quoted quite extensively from the texts of Islaam. In quoting verses from the *Qur'aan*, I have avoided using archaic English as is found in some Biblical and Qur'aanic translations, as it tends to render some of the subject matter obscure. What has been written below the Arabic verses found in this book is a "translation of the meaning" of the *Qur'aan*, as opposed to a literal translation.

In certain rare instances, I have included some verses from the Old and New Testaments. Muslims believe in the scriptures that were given to the former prophets. However, they do not believe that the scriptures that are in circulation today amongst the present day Jews and Christians are exactly the same as they were when they were originally revealed. Consequently, Muslims neither accept nor reject their contents, unless a matter can be confirmed or negated by a verse of the *Qur'aan* or an authentic *hadeeth* (prophetic narration).

It is my hope that this book will contribute to a better understanding of Islaam, and I welcome any kind of feedback from anyone who finds any points of contention within it.

Haneef Oliver
1425/7/6
21/08/2004

Why Do Muslims Reject Atheism?

People's Beliefs About the Existence of God

Atheism can be described as the belief that no creator exists, and that the universe was not brought about by divine knowledge, will and ability. Although many famous people have claimed to be atheists or agnostics[2] throughout history, they have often been found to be a minority within their communities.

On October 16, 2003, Opinion Dynamics Corporation released a national poll showing that "92 percent of Americans say they believe in God."[3] Indeed, a large portion of mankind affirms some kind of belief in the existence of God, as this is something that is known to mankind by way of the natural disposition that God has given mankind to know instinctively about His existence, and that He was the cause of their coming to being.[4]

Even those few who deny the existence of God, do so only by covering up this natural disposition which they were given, allowing pride and doubt to dominate their instinctive awareness of their Creator. This was the case of the Pharaoh who oppressed Moses (ﷺ)[5] and the Children of Israel. Pharaoh not only denied the existence of Allaah,[6] but he also claimed to

---

[2] An agnostic has been defined as "a person who is not sure whether or not God exists." (Oxford Advanced Learner's Dictionary, Oxford University Press, Walton Street, Oxford, 1995, p. 582.)

[3] Dana Blanton, More Believe In God Than Heaven, *FOX News*, October 16, 2003.

[4] Mankind was given this instinctive awareness of their Creator. However, the details of how to worship and obey Him do not come by way of this *fitrah*, but instead, by way of revelation.

[5] *'Alayhis-Salaam* is a supplication that a Muslim repeats after mentioning the name of a prophet, which means, "Peace be upon him."

[6] Although most Westerners refer to the Creator by using the word God, English speakers have actually only used this word as a substitute for the true name of the Creator that He revealed in His books. The name of the Creator in the Bible has been transliterated into the English language as El, Elah, Elohim (expressed in the plural

=

be the Lord of the worlds. In the final revelation given to mankind, Allaah said:

﴿ فَحَشَرَ فَنَادَىٰ ﴿٢٣﴾ فَقَالَ أَنَا۠ رَبُّكُمُ ٱلۡأَعۡلَىٰ ﴿٢٤﴾ ﴾

Then he (Pharaoh) gathered (his people) and called out, saying, "I am your Lord, Most High."
[79:24]

This statement by Pharaoh was not made out of true conviction, but rather, out of arrogance:

﴿ وَجَحَدُواْ بِهَا وَٱسۡتَيۡقَنَتۡهَآ أَنفُسُهُمۡ ظُلۡمٗا وَعُلُوّٗاۚ فَٱنظُرۡ كَيۡفَ كَانَ عَٰقِبَةُ ٱلۡمُفۡسِدِينَ ﴿١٤﴾ ﴾

And they rejected those Signs in iniquity and arrogance, though their souls were convinced thereof: So see what was the end of those who acted corruptly.
[27:14]

Pharaoh's arrogance was swiftly terminated when Allaah parted the sea for Moses (عليه السلام) and his followers, and Pharaoh was made to see that he was going to die, and meet the One whom he denied:

﴿ ۞ وَجَٰوَزۡنَا بِبَنِيٓ إِسۡرَٰٓءِيلَ ٱلۡبَحۡرَ فَأَتۡبَعَهُمۡ فِرۡعَوۡنُ وَجُنُودُهُۥ بَغۡيٗا وَعَدۡوًاۖ حَتَّىٰٓ إِذَآ أَدۡرَكَهُ ٱلۡغَرَقُ قَالَ ءَامَنتُ أَنَّهُۥ لَآ إِلَٰهَ إِلَّا ٱلَّذِيٓ ءَامَنَتۡ بِهِۦ بَنُوٓاْ إِسۡرَٰٓءِيلَ وَأَنَا۠ مِنَ ٱلۡمُسۡلِمِينَ ﴿٩٠﴾ ءَآلۡـَٰٔنَ وَقَدۡ عَصَيۡتَ قَبۡلُ وَكُنتَ مِنَ ٱلۡمُفۡسِدِينَ ﴿٩١﴾ فَٱلۡيَوۡمَ نُنَجِّيكَ بِبَدَنِكَ لِتَكُونَ لِمَنۡ خَلۡفَكَ ءَايَةٗۚ وَإِنَّ كَثِيرٗا مِّنَ ٱلنَّاسِ عَنۡ ءَايَٰتِنَا لَغَٰفِلُونَ ﴿٩٢﴾ ﴾

form to convey His grandeur; this word is taken from the singular form Eloh), Eloah, Eli and Eloi. The Aramaic name for the Creator is Alah. In summary, the roots and meanings of all these transliterations are essentially the same. El, Eli, Eloi, Eloh, Eloah, Elah, Alah, Allah, or Allaah; all of these words are human efforts at transliterating the true name of the Creator from Semitic languages to the English language.

We took the Children of Israel across the sea; Pharaoh and his hosts followed them in oppression and enmity, till when drowning overtook him, he said: "I believe that none has the right to be worshipped but He in Whom the Children of Israel believe, and I am one of those who submit (to His Will in Islaam)."

Now (you believe)? And you had disobeyed (Us) before, and were one of the corrupting evildoers.

So this day We shall deliver your (dead) body (out from the sea) that you may be a Sign to those who come after you. And verily, many among mankind are heedless of Our Signs.
[10:90-92]

Likewise, when faced with life or death situations such as being in a plane that is about to crash, those who claim to be agnostics or atheists often find themselves instinctively supplicating to their Creator to relieve them of their distress. Their resorting to pray to their Creator only occurs when all other worldly means have been exhausted, knowing that no pilot, motor or parachute can help them. This is the time they lift the veil of self-deceit and turn to their Creator alone, although it was their Creator who had always been controlling all the affairs they had previously been relying on.

﴿ قُلْ مَن يُنَجِّيكُم مِّن ظُلُمَٰتِ ٱلْبَرِّ وَٱلْبَحْرِ تَدْعُونَهُۥ تَضَرُّعًا وَخُفْيَةً لَّئِنْ أَنجَىٰنَا مِنْ هَٰذِهِۦ لَنَكُونَنَّ مِنَ ٱلشَّٰكِرِينَ ﴿٦٣﴾ قُلِ ٱللَّهُ يُنَجِّيكُم مِّنْهَا وَمِن كُلِّ كَرْبٍ ثُمَّ أَنتُمْ تُشْرِكُونَ ﴿٦٤﴾ ﴾

Say (to them, O Muhammad)**: "Who is it that delivers you from the dark recesses of land and sea, when you call upon Him in humility and silent terror: 'If He only delivers us from these (dangers), (we vow) we shall truly show our gratitude?'"**

Say: "Allaah rescues you from this and from all (other) distresses, then you worship others besides Him."
[6:63-64]

When these people who claimed they were agnostics or atheists single out Allaah, praying to Him in their dire time of need, they suddenly come to the realization that He exists, and that only He can help them. This realization comes about as a result of their awareness that Allaah is the

One who possesses all power and ability as regards all things, that He is all encompassing, fully acquainted with them, and controlling their affairs.

Signs of the Creator's Existence

To illustrate this necessary conclusion, a simple analogy can be drawn. Prosecutors are known to bring forward evidences such as DNA samples, footprints and fingerprints, to find people guilty of certain crimes that nobody has actually witnessed. Just as footprints in the ground point to the fact that a person had once walked in that place, examining Allaah's Signs within His creational arrangement proves conclusively that every single thing that exists within the universe came about by a Most Wise Creator.

Indeed, one can come to this realization by turning to the created things and reflecting upon their nature, in order to conclude that they did not come about by themselves. Only One who possesses infinite knowledge and the capability to create would be able to bring the universe and all it contains into being, and to balance and administrate all of its affairs in such a stable manner.

Allaah invites mankind to reflect upon the creation and its sophistication in order to conclude that only a Most Wise and knowledgeable Creator created them, and that as such, nothing deserves to be worshipped or served except Him:

﴿ إِنَّ فِي خَلْقِ ٱلسَّمَٰوَٰتِ وَٱلْأَرْضِ وَٱخْتِلَٰفِ
ٱلَّيْلِ وَٱلنَّهَارِ لَءَايَٰتٍ لِّأُو۟لِى ٱلْأَلْبَٰبِ ١٩٠ ﴾

Verily, in the creation of the heavens and the earth, and in the alternation of night and day, there are indeed Signs for men of understanding.
[3:190]

Shaykh 'Abdur-Razzaaaq al'Abbaad, a contemporary academic, said: "Contemplate the night and day; they are amongst the most amazing Signs of Allaah. See how He made the night for resting and as a covering. It envelops the world causing the cessation of activities. Animals retire to their dwellings and the birds to their nests. The souls relax and take rest from the pains of their labour and fatigue until when the souls are reposed and have slept, they now look forward to their livelihood and its disposal. The

Splitter of the morning (ﷻ) brings forward the day, His army giving glad tidings of the (coming of) the morning. It vanquishes that darkness and tears it asunder, unveiling the darkness from the world. Thereafter, the inhabitants are able to see. The animals then circulate about the land and proceed to manage their livelihood and welfare, and the birds depart from their nests. What a returning and arising, which is so indicative of Allaah's capability (to assemble the creation) for the Major Return.[7]

Now ponder over the delicate and fine air that is held captive between the sky and earth. It is sensed through feeling when it blows; its substance is felt but its form cannot be seen. It runs between the sky and earth; the birds circle and fly in it, swimming with their wings just as the fish of the sea swim in water. Its sides and gusts collide against each other when in commotion, just as the waves of the ocean clash.

Consider how Allaah (ﷻ) forms with this wind, clouds that are held between the sky and earth. The wind excites the clouds causing them to rise and become dense. Allaah then combines the clouds together and merges them, and drives them by the wind to the land in need (of rain).

When they rise and ascend above the land, their water falls upon it. Allaah dispatches the winds whilst the clouds are in the atmosphere. The winds scatter and separate the clouds so that they do not harm or destroy what they would if the water were to descend upon it all at once. Once the land takes its fill and need, the clouds leave off the land and disperse. Thus, these clouds water the earth and are carried by the winds."[8]

The light of day is also an astounding Sign of a great Creator. Dangerous ultraviolet and infrared radiation are highly absorbed by the earth's atmosphere, thus protecting mankind from being exposed to, and harmed by them. In contrast, sunlight that is necessary for mankind's existence is allowed to pass through the earth's atmosphere. Is this an accident?

If the sun were any closer to the earth, heat and radiation would destroy us, and conversely, if the sun were any farther from the earth, all life would cease. An incredibly complex equilibrium is constantly maintained in all affairs, and amazingly, the laws that govern this equilibrium main-

[7] The Day of Resurrection and Judgement

[8] Shaykh 'Abdur-Razzaaq al-'Abbaad, *Asbaab Ziyaadatil-Eemaan wa Nuqsaanihi, Ghiraas lin-Nashr wat-Tawzi'*, pp.40-41.

tain the same unity throughout the whole universe. Could this possibly have occurred through a process of random self-assembly?

Those who believe in chance concede that it is something which is not by nature ordered. Once this is understood, the following question must be asked: **How could something that is by nature disordered consistently create order?** This is a scientific impossibility. Hence, it must be concluded that not only has a Creator created our universe, but that He is also continually administrating its awe-inspiring affairs.

A Revealing Illustration

To demonstrate the error of those who deny the existence of a Creator, one may consider the ordinary example of how a book comes into being. The existence of a book necessitates the existence of a publisher who possesses three attributes: Firstly, this publisher must possess the **knowledge** of the required fields of expertise for the production of this book. Secondly, the publisher must possess the **will** to carry out such a task by consciously embarking upon this project. Thirdly, the publisher must possess the **ability** to carry out the task of creating the pages, cover and binding of the book while finishing it with distinction.

Once this is understood, the irrationality of claiming that a book created itself, or that it came about by mere chance, becomes apparent. Is it possible to legitimately claim that a book came about without a publisher, or that this universe came about without a Creator - solely on the basis that this publisher or Creator has not been seen?

In actuality, understanding that a Creator exists is much easier to grasp than understanding that a simple object like a book has an originator, as the formation of our universe is far more sophisticated than the formation of any one particular object. Accordingly, the Creator stated regarding those who deny His existence:

﴿ أَمْ خُلِقُوا۟ مِنْ غَيْرِ شَىْءٍ أَمْ هُمُ ٱلْخَـٰلِقُونَ ﴿٣٥﴾
أَمْ خَلَقُوا۟ ٱلسَّمَـٰوَٰتِ وَٱلْأَرْضَ ۚ بَل لَّا يُوقِنُونَ ﴿٣٦﴾ ﴾

"Were they created by nothing, or were they themselves the creators?
Or did they create the heavens and the earth?
Nay, they have no firm belief."
[52:35-36]

These verses prove that just as it would be impossible to claim that a book was created by nothing, it would also be impossible to claim that mankind was created by nothing. Likewise, just as it would be impossible to claim that a book created itself, it would also be impossible to claim that we created ourselves. Only one other possibility exists; that mankind and everything in this universe was brought about by an All-Knowing Creator.

It can be concluded that all things are known to come into existence by designers that possess the three attributes of **knowledge**, **will** and **ability** to create. No other conclusion can be drawn, except that our universe was fashioned by a Creator who possesses the **knowledge**, **will** and **ability** to create such an incredibly awe-inspiring formation.

Indeed, certain pieces of evidence left behind at the scene of a crime are considered incriminating proofs that lead courts to settle cases in an absolute manner. In the same way, Allaah's Signs within His creation and the logical evidences contained within His revelation contain even more definite proofs that we were created by an All-Knowing, All-Powerful God.

﴿ وَفِي ٱلْأَرْضِ ءَايَـٰتٌ لِّلْمُوقِنِينَ ﴿٢٠﴾ وَفِيٓ أَنفُسِكُمْ ۚ أَفَلَا تُبْصِرُونَ ﴿٢١﴾ ﴾

"And upon the earth are Signs visible to all who have faith with certainty, just as there are Signs within your own selves. Will you not then see?"
[51:20,21]

Why Do Muslims Reject Worshipping Others Along With God?

Ingratitude

Once one accepts that a Creator exists, who alone, is continually creating, sustaining and administrating the universe, it becomes logically obvious that those who worship and serve the Creator alone, do so in truth. Indeed, would it be reasonable to affirm the Oneness of the Creator in His creational and administrative capabilities, and then proceed to worship and serve others along with Him?

﴿ ذَٰلِكَ بِأَنَّ ٱللَّهَ هُوَ ٱلْحَقُّ وَأَنَّ مَا يَدْعُونَ مِن دُونِهِۦ هُوَ ٱلْبَـٰطِلُ وَأَنَّ ٱللَّهَ هُوَ ٱلْعَلِىُّ ٱلْكَبِيرُ ﴿٦٢﴾ ﴾

That is because Allaah - He is the Truth,[9] and what they invoke besides Him is falsehood. And verily, Allaah - He is the Most High, the Most Great.
[22:62]

In the final revelation sent down to mankind, the Creator clarified that He deserves to be worshipped alone, as well as why this is the case.[10] Simi-

---

[9] The only True God of all that exists, who has no partners or rivals along with Him; neither in His creational capabilities, nor in His right to be worshipped alone.

[10] All of the Prophets followed a clear and set methodology in making monotheism the starting and ending point of their call. The Old Testament is full of verses that call for the singling out of Allaah in all worship. In Deuteronomy 6:13, it is mentioned that only God alone should be served: "Fear the Lord your God, **serve Him only** and take your oaths in His name."

Hosea 13:4 states that there is no other God who saves His servants from His punishment except Him: "I am the Lord your God who brought you out of Egypt. **You shall acknowledge no God but me, no saviour except me.**"

=

larly, He has also clarified the state of those who worship others besides Him, such as stars, trees, idols, angels, prophets, pious people and the like. He has shown how these objects of worship never created anything that might justify their being worshipped and served. On the contrary, they existed for a limited period, and faded as a subject of creation, bound by the laws of the Creator.

After reminding us about all the creational favours He has provided, our Creator asks us in the following verses whether we would be able to create any of the wondrous matters of His creation that He originated from nothing. Furthermore, we are asked whether it is befitting that the countless gods and goddesses that are raised and then forgotten about throughout the ages should receive any kind of devotion after all He has provided for us:

﴿ أَمَّنْ خَلَقَ ٱلسَّمَٰوَٰتِ وَٱلْأَرْضَ وَأَنزَلَ لَكُم مِّنَ ٱلسَّمَآءِ مَآءً فَأَنۢبَتْنَا بِهِۦ حَدَآئِقَ ذَاتَ بَهْجَةٍ مَّا كَانَ لَكُمْ أَن تُنۢبِتُوا۟ شَجَرَهَآ ۗ أَءِلَٰهٌ مَّعَ ٱللَّهِ ۚ بَلْ هُمْ قَوْمٌ يَعْدِلُونَ ﴿٦٠﴾ ﴾

Is not He Who created the heavens and the earth, and sends down for you rain from the sky, whereby We cause to grow wonderful gardens full of beauty and delight, (better than the gods you worship)? It is not in your ability to cause the growth of their trees.

Although there do exist some verses in the New Testament which imply divinity for Jesus (عليه السلام), these verses clearly contradict many other verses, in which Jesus (عليه السلام) is reported to have affirmed divinity only for the One who sent him as a prophet, not as a god: "And this is the life eternal, that they might know thee, **the only true God and Jesus whom you have sent.**" (John 17:3)

The existence of a minority of verses in the New Testament attributing divine status to Jesus (عليه السلام) can be attributed to later additions which dishonest priests and scribes added to the original texts. The call of each prophet was not that *they* be worshipped, but rather, to tell the people, **"Worship Allaah: You have no other god but Him."** (The *Qur'aan* 23:32)

Jesus did not differ from the prophets who came before him, as he fulfilled his responsibility of telling mankind about monotheism. What is found in the *Qur'aan*, namely, **"None deserves to be worshipped or served except Him,"** is what Jesus (عليه السلام) and all the prophets taught. It was only those who came after Jesus who changed his message: "For it is written: **Worship the Lord your God, and serve Him only.**" (Matthew 4:10)

Is there any god along with Allaah?
Nay, but they are a people who ascribe equals (with Him).

﴿ أَمَّن جَعَلَ ٱلْأَرْضَ قَرَارًا وَجَعَلَ خِلَٰلَهَآ أَنْهَٰرًا وَجَعَلَ لَهَا رَوَٰسِىَ وَجَعَلَ بَيْنَ
ٱلْبَحْرَيْنِ حَاجِزًا ۗ أَءِلَٰهٌ مَّعَ ٱللَّهِ ۚ بَلْ أَكْثَرُهُمْ لَا يَعْلَمُونَ ٦١ ﴾

Is not He Who has made the earth as a fixed abode, and has placed rivers in its midst, and has placed firm mountains therein, and has set a barrier between the two seas (of salt and sweet water), (better than the gods you worship)?
Is there any god along with Allaah?
Nay, but most of them know not.

﴿ أَمَّن يُجِيبُ ٱلْمُضْطَرَّ إِذَا دَعَاهُ وَيَكْشِفُ ٱلسُّوٓءَ وَيَجْعَلُكُمْ خُلَفَآءَ
ٱلْأَرْضِ ۗ أَءِلَٰهٌ مَّعَ ٱللَّهِ ۚ قَلِيلًا مَّا تَذَكَّرُونَ ٦٢ ﴾

Is not He Who responds to the distressed one, when he calls on Him, and Who removes the evil, and makes you inheritors of the earth, generations after generations, (better than the gods you worship)?
Is there any god along with Allaah?
Little it is that you remember.

﴿ أَمَّن يَهْدِيكُمْ فِى ظُلُمَٰتِ ٱلْبَرِّ وَٱلْبَحْرِ وَمَن يُرْسِلُ ٱلرِّيَٰحَ بُشْرًۢا بَيْنَ يَدَىْ
رَحْمَتِهِۦٓ ۗ أَءِلَٰهٌ مَّعَ ٱللَّهِ ۚ تَعَٰلَى ٱللَّهُ عَمَّا يُشْرِكُونَ ٦٣ ﴾

Is not He Who guides you in the darkness of the land and the sea, and Who sends the winds as heralds of glad tidings, going before His Mercy [rain], **(better than the gods you worship)?**
Is there any god along with Allaah?
High and Exalted is Allaah above all that they associate as partners (with Him).

﴿ أَمَّن يَبْدَؤُا۟ ٱلْخَلْقَ ثُمَّ يُعِيدُهُۥ وَمَن يَرْزُقُكُم مِّنَ ٱلسَّمَآءِ وَٱلْأَرْضِ ۗ
أَءِلَٰهٌ مَّعَ ٱللَّهِ ۚ قُلْ هَاتُوا۟ بُرْهَٰنَكُمْ إِن كُنتُمْ صَٰدِقِينَ ٦٤ ﴾

Is not He Who originates creation, and shall thereafter repeat it,
and Who provides for you from heaven and earth,
(better than the gods you worship)?
Is there any god along with Allaah?
Say (to them):
"Bring forth your proofs, if you are truthful."
[27:60-64]

The Greatest Crime Imaginable

People concede that crimes which are perpetrated against the creation can be great in nature. How much greater then, must the level of crime be, if it is perpetrated against the One who brought these forms of creation into being?

﴿ كَيْفَ تَكْفُرُونَ بِٱللَّهِ وَكُنتُمْ أَمْوَٰتًا فَأَحْيَٰكُمْ ۖ ثُمَّ يُمِيتُكُمْ ثُمَّ يُحْيِيكُمْ ثُمَّ إِلَيْهِ تُرْجَعُونَ ٢٨ ﴾

How can you disbelieve in Allaah? Seeing that you were dead and He gave you life; then He will cause you to die, then again will bring you to life (on the Day of Resurrection); then unto Him you will return.
[2:28]

Indeed, it has been clarified in the *Qur'aan* that the greatest crime someone can commit is to attribute partners to the One who possesses absolute power and control over the universe. This crime is perpetrated when people worship and serve others along with God after He has mercifully provided for them in uncountable ways.

Contemplate the countless favours our Creator has provided for mankind, such as the blessing of gravity. This incredible force is perfectly balanced, preventing us from either floating in the air, or being too weighted down to the ground. Likewise, profound reflection upon the uncounted blessing of how our lungs and heart extract oxygen from the air point to the all-encompassing nature of our Creator's wisdom, capability and generosity towards us. Through the process of respiration, our cardiovascular system is able to function, keeping us alive and well. Interestingly, it is not impossible for someone to expect their heart to function for a period of approximately seventy years, yet we do not expect an engine to function without rest for even a portion of this time.

Consider the miraculous nature of our digestive system and how it breaks down all the necessary components of food that we need. Distributing necessary nutrients to our body, it also expels any harmful wastes. Furthermore, the intestinal bacteria that exist in our digestive tract constitute an important part of our immune system, which fights off disease and infection.

Indeed, the balance and control of the components of every atom within ourselves not only indicate the existence of a Creator, but also attest to the great favours He continually bestows upon us. Mankind tends to be ungrateful for these favours, either by being unmindful of them, or by refusing to acknowledge them to begin with.

﴿ أَفَبِٱلْبَـٰطِلِ يُؤْمِنُونَ وَبِنِعْمَتِ ٱللَّهِ هُمْ يَكْفُرُونَ ﴾

Do they then believe in falsehood, and deny the favours of Allaah?
[16:72]

The discerning are able to ponder over the uncountable favours Allaah has bestowed upon them and appreciate the excellence of their arrangements, their beauty and their perfection. However, every kind of perfection that can be witnessed in these creations is incomparable with the perfection of the Creator. Those who come to this realization understand that all these creational favours call to the glorification of their originator, gratitude and attachment to Him, and sincerity in singling Him out in all forms of worship and servitude.

Nevertheless, even if a person were to attempt to establish every kind of worship known in a continuous fashion, never would this individual be able to fulfill the gratitude the Creator deserves for these favours. For this reason, God is Oft-Forgiving, Most Merciful, and is pleased with only an undemanding amount of thankfulness, while He provides much.

﴿ وَإِن تَعُدُّوا۟ نِعْمَةَ ٱللَّهِ لَا تُحْصُوهَآ ۗ إِنَّ ٱللَّهَ لَغَفُورٌ رَّحِيمٌ ﴿١٨﴾ ﴾

And if you would count the favours of Allaah, never would you be able to enumerate them. Truly, Allaah is Oft-Forgiving, Most Merciful.
[16:18]

The One who has provided us with the faculties of hearing, seeing and understanding has explained that worshipping and serving others along with God constitutes an immense form of ingratitude. This is especially so when understanding that these objects of worship never played any part in originating any of these favours. Consequently, it is the only sin that will never be forgiven if a person dies in such a state without repenting:

﴿ إِنَّ ٱللَّهَ لَا يَغْفِرُ أَن يُشْرَكَ بِهِۦ وَيَغْفِرُ مَا دُونَ ذَٰلِكَ لِمَن يَشَآءُ ۚ وَمَن يُشْرِكْ بِٱللَّهِ فَقَدِ ٱفْتَرَىٰٓ إِثْمًا عَظِيمًا ﴿٤٨﴾ ﴾

Verily, Allaah forgives not that partners should be set up with Him (in worship), but He forgives what is less than that for whom He wills; and whoever sets up partners with Allaah in worship, has indeed invented a tremendous sin.

[4:48]

Many Christians believe that the Prophet Jesus (عليه السلام) was part of a trinity, and as such, is worthy of being worshipped along with God. Christians are not alone in this kind of deification. Some people who ascribe themselves to Islaam have deified individuals who are of much lesser standing than Jesus (عليه السلام). Upon reflection, it can be realized that none of these individuals, no matter how great or pious they were, are deserving of any share of worship.

﴿ مَّا ٱلْمَسِيحُ ٱبْنُ مَرْيَمَ إِلَّا رَسُولٌ قَدْ خَلَتْ مِن قَبْلِهِ ٱلرُّسُلُ وَأُمُّهُۥ صِدِّيقَةٌ ۖ كَانَا يَأْكُلَانِ ٱلطَّعَامَ ۗ ٱنظُرْ كَيْفَ نُبَيِّنُ لَهُمُ ٱلْـَٔايَـٰتِ ثُمَّ ٱنظُرْ أَنَّىٰ يُؤْفَكُونَ ﴿٧٥﴾ ﴾

The Messiah (Jesus) son of Mary was no more than a Messenger; many were the Messengers that passed away before him. His mother was a woman of truth.[11] They both used to eat food.[12] Look how We make the Signs clear to them, yet look how they are deluded away (from the truth).

[5:75]

[11] Meaning: She believed in the words of Allaah and His Books.

[12] Meaning: They both used to eat food as any other human being, while Allaah does not need sustenance. If Jesus used to eat food, it would not make logical sense to believe that he is part of a divine trinity, or that he be called the Lord, or that he be worshipped along with God.

Not only are these things or people that are worshipped besides God incapable of creating anything, they cannot even hear the invocations that people make to them. Consequently, these objects of worship can neither benefit them nor harm them.

﴿ وَمَنْ أَضَلُّ مِمَّن يَدْعُواْ مِن دُونِ ٱللَّهِ مَن لَّا يَسْتَجِيبُ لَهُۥٓ إِلَىٰ يَوْمِ ٱلْقِيَٰمَةِ وَهُمْ عَن دُعَآئِهِمْ غَٰفِلُونَ ﴿٥﴾ ﴾

And who is more astray than he who invokes besides Allaah, those who will not answer him until the Day of Resurrection, and are not even aware of their being called upon?
[46:5]

The View of Liberalist Ideologies Towards Polytheism

According to liberalist ideologies, these types of polytheistic transgressions towards the Creator are not recognized as crimes. On the contrary, they are encouraged, and those who take part in them are considered to be the same as anyone else, or often deemed better than others. On the other hand, those who closely follow the way of the prophets and single out the Creator in all worship and obedience are considered to be backwards and misguided.

﴿ أَمَّنْ هُوَ قَٰنِتٌ ءَانَآءَ ٱلَّيْلِ سَاجِدًا وَقَآئِمًا يَحْذَرُ ٱلْأَخِرَةَ وَيَرْجُواْ رَحْمَةَ رَبِّهِۦ ۗ قُلْ هَلْ يَسْتَوِى ٱلَّذِينَ يَعْلَمُونَ وَٱلَّذِينَ لَا يَعْلَمُونَ ۗ إِنَّمَا يَتَذَكَّرُ أُوْلُواْ ٱلْأَلْبَٰبِ ﴿٩﴾ ﴾

Is one who is obedient to Allaah, prostrating himself and standing (in prayer) during the hours of the night, fearing the hereafter and hoping for the Mercy of his Lord, (like one who disbelieves)? Say (to them): "Are they the same; those who know and those who do not?" Only those who are endowed with understanding will receive admonition.
[39:9]

Can Mankind Rightfully Formulate Their Own Religion?

A World Without True Meaning

Existentialism is the theory that human beings "are free and responsible for their own actions in a world without meaning or God."[13] Although many liberalists would not like to openly state they believe that life has no meaning or that there is no God, a closer examination of their beliefs shows they agree with some of the principles of existentialism. Many liberalists hold that there is no absolute truth to be followed in life, and that God exists, but should be relegated to only a minimal, private aspect of mankind's lives.

On November 27, 2001, *The New York Times'* Thomas Friedman conformed to these principles when he made the statement that God "is not exhausted by just one faith." Friedman's reason for holding this pluralistic belief is based upon the fact that "God speaks multiple languages." Friedman is truly representative of this popular mode of thinking in his criticism of what he terms "exclusivist religious visions." In an effort to support this criticism, Friedman states that God "speaks Arabic on Fridays, Hebrew on Saturdays and Latin on Sundays."

﴿ وَمِنَ ٱلنَّاسِ مَن يُجَـٰدِلُ فِى ٱللَّهِ بِغَيْرِ عِلْمٍ وَلَا هُدًى وَلَا كِتَـٰبٍ مُّنِيرٍ ﴿٨﴾ ﴾

And among men is he who disputes about Allaah without knowledge, without guidance, and without a Book of Enlightenment.

[22:8]

Ultimately denying that Allaah is capable of sending down true revelation or that He has a specific will for His creation, Friedman continued his pluralist call with the romantically charged notion that God "welcomes

---

[13] Oxford Advanced Learner's Dictionary, Oxford University Press, Walton Street, Oxford, 1995, p. 403.

different human beings approaching him through their own history, out of their language and cultural heritage."[14] In short, Friedman believes that human beings are free to do as they like in a world without absolute truth or meaning, with each individual formulating their own truth and meaning to life.

One God, One Way

This pluralistic pretext can also be witnessed in the commonly held belief that there are "three Abrahamic faiths of Christianity, Islam and Judaism."[15] Although it is a popular contemporary belief to state that there are three Abrahamic faiths, in actuality, the Bible does not contain any instruction to enter into a religion called Judaism or Christianity. Noah (ﷺ), Abraham (ﷺ), Ishmael (ﷺ), Isaac (ﷺ) and Jacob (ﷺ) came before the words Judaism and Christianity even existed.

﴿ مَا كَانَ إِبْرَٰهِيمُ يَهُودِيًّا وَلَا نَصْرَانِيًّا وَلَـٰكِن كَانَ
حَنِيفًا مُّسْلِمًا وَمَا كَانَ مِنَ ٱلْمُشْرِكِينَ ﴿٦٧﴾ ﴾

"Abraham was neither a Jew nor a Christian, but he was *Haneefan Musliman* [an upright Monotheist who submitted himself to Allaah]**, and he was not of those who associated partners with Allaah in worship."**

[3:67]

For this reason, the One who sent Abraham as a prophet addressed those who would dispute this matter, saying:

﴿ يَـٰٓأَهْلَ ٱلْكِتَـٰبِ لِمَ تُحَآجُّونَ فِىٓ إِبْرَٰهِيمَ وَمَآ أُنزِلَتِ ٱلتَّوْرَىٰةُ
وَٱلْإِنجِيلُ إِلَّا مِنۢ بَعْدِهِۦٓ ۚ أَفَلَا تَعْقِلُونَ ﴿٦٥﴾ ﴾

O people of the Scripture![16] Why do you dispute about Abraham, while the Torah and the Gospel were not revealed till after him? Have you then no sense?

[3:65]

[14] Thomas L. Friedman, The Real War, *New York Times*, November 27, 2001.

[15] Chris Herlinger, Faiths probe forces of evil, *The Sun Herald*, May 21, 2004.

[16] Jews and Christians

Consequently, there is no such thing as three Abrahamic faiths, as Abraham and his descendants only had one system of belief, which was the way of his Creator. All of the prophets were commanded to submit to the One God worthy of all worship, and to follow His single way. In Arabic, this form of submission is called Islaam, a comprehensive word chosen by the Creator to allude to the act of submitting to Him and following His message.

﴿ وَمَن يَرْغَبُ عَن مِّلَّةِ إِبْرَٰهِـۧمَ إِلَّا مَن سَفِهَ نَفْسَهُۥ ۚ وَلَقَدِ ٱصْطَفَيْنَٰهُ فِى ٱلدُّنْيَا ۖ
وَإِنَّهُۥ فِى ٱلْـَٔاخِرَةِ لَمِنَ ٱلصَّٰلِحِينَ ﴿١٣٠﴾ إِذْ قَالَ لَهُۥ رَبُّهُۥٓ أَسْلِمْ ۖ قَالَ أَسْلَمْتُ لِرَبِّ
ٱلْعَٰلَمِينَ ﴿١٣١﴾ وَوَصَّىٰ بِهَآ إِبْرَٰهِـۧمُ بَنِيهِ وَيَعْقُوبُ يَٰبَنِىَّ إِنَّ ٱللَّهَ ٱصْطَفَىٰ
لَكُمُ ٱلدِّينَ فَلَا تَمُوتُنَّ إِلَّا وَأَنتُم مُّسْلِمُونَ ﴿١٣٢﴾ ﴾

And who turns away from the religion of Abraham except one who befools himself? Truly, We chose him in this world and verily, in the Hereafter, he will be among the righteous.

(Remember) when his Lord said to him, "*Aslim* (submit)."[17] He said, "I have submitted (in Islaam) to the Lord of the worlds."

And Abraham instructed his sons (to submit in Islaam), and (so did) Jacob, (saying), "O my sons, indeed Allaah has chosen for you this religion, so do not die except as Muslims (i.e. those who have submitted themselves to God)."
[2:130-132]

All of the Prophets taught the same message of submission to the One God. Not only was the essence of their call the same, many matters of worship were also very similar from one prophet to another.[18] However,

---

[17] *Aslim* is the command from the Arabic verb *aslama*, and the word Islaam and Muslim all stem from this verb of submitting or surrendering oneself to God.

[18] Muslims are commanded to make ablution (ceremonial washing) before they pray, just as the former nations were too. With time, these nations left the way of their messengers, and consequently, have lost this and other forms of worship:

"And he set the laver between the tent of the meeting and the altar, and put water in it for washing, with which Moses and Aaron and his sons washed their hands and their feet...as the Lord commanded Moses." (Exodus 40:30-31)

=

different laws were revealed to different prophets, according to the wisdom of the Knower of all things. This unity of religion was only affected after later followers of the prophets changed the messages they were given and separated into different religions and sects. This splitting caused each religion and sect to name itself with a new name, as well as to envy the other religions and sects that differed with them:

﴿ إِنَّ ٱلدِّينَ عِندَ ٱللَّهِ ٱلْإِسْلَـٰمُ ۗ وَمَا ٱخْتَلَفَ ٱلَّذِينَ أُوتُوا۟ ٱلْكِتَـٰبَ إِلَّا مِنۢ بَعْدِ مَا جَآءَهُمُ ٱلْعِلْمُ بَغْيًۢا بَيْنَهُمْ ۗ وَمَن يَكْفُرْ بِـَٔايَـٰتِ ٱللَّهِ فَإِنَّ ٱللَّهَ سَرِيعُ ٱلْحِسَابِ ﴾

Truly, the religion before Allaah is Islaam (submission to Him). Those who were given the Scripture did not differ except out of mutual jealousy, after knowledge had come to them. And whoever disbelieves in the Signs of Allaah, then surely, Allaah is swift in calling to account.
[3:19]

Muslims bow, kneel, and prostrate in their prayer, just as the former prophets and their followers had:

"O come, let us worship and bow down: let us kneel before the Lord our maker." (Psalms 95:6)

"When Abraham was ninety-nine years old the Lord appeared to Abraham, and said to him, 'I am God Almighty; walk before me, and be blameless. And I will make my covenant between me and you, and will multiply you exceedingly.' **Then Abraham fell on his face.**" (Genesis 17:1-3)

"Then Jehoshaphat **bowed his head with his face to the ground**, and all Judah and the inhabitants of Jerusalem fell down before the Lord, worshiping the Lord." (2Chronicals 20:18.8)

"And **Joshua fell on his face** to the earth, and did worship." (Joshua 5:14)

"... and they [Moses and Aaron] **fell upon their faces**: and the glory of the Lord appeared upon them." (Numbers 20:6)

Most present-day Jews and Christians today find the act of prostrating to be foreign and even contemptible, even though their Prophets and their true followers worshipped Allaah in this manner. However, for Muslims, prostrating before Allaah is the pinnacle of servitude to him, because it shows that the Muslim has submitted him or herself completely to the Creator, which is the essence of Islaam. The New Testament states that Jesus prostrated and submitted himself to God: "And he went a little further and **fell on his face and prayed.**'" (Matthew 26:39)

No matter how attached people might be to the religions and ways they have inherited, it would not make sense to believe that the Creator recognizes any religion except the one He has revealed:

﴿ وَمَن يَبْتَغِ غَيْرَ ٱلْإِسْلَٰمِ دِينًا فَلَن يُقْبَلَ مِنْهُ وَهُوَ فِى ٱلْءَاخِرَةِ مِنَ ٱلْخَٰسِرِينَ ﴿٨٥﴾ ﴾

And whoever seeks a religion other than Islaam, it will never be accepted of him, and in the Hereafter he will be one of the losers.
[3:85]

Contrary to the principles of pluralism, the Creator has clarified His will that mankind adhere to His one, chosen way:

﴿ وَأَنَّ هَٰذَا صِرَٰطِى مُسْتَقِيمًا فَٱتَّبِعُوهُ ۖ وَلَا تَتَّبِعُوا۟ ٱلسُّبُلَ فَتَفَرَّقَ بِكُمْ عَن سَبِيلِهِۦ ۚ ذَٰلِكُمْ وَصَّىٰكُم بِهِۦ لَعَلَّكُمْ تَتَّقُونَ ﴿١٥٣﴾ ﴾

And verily, this is My Straight Way, so follow it, and follow not (other) ways, for they will separate you away from His Way. This He has ordained for you, that you may become righteous and dutiful.
[6:153]

Allaah said that this is **"My Straight Way,"** and that mankind should **"follow it."** He did not say, "These are My Multiple Ways." Rather, He said, **"And verily, this is My Straight Way."**

It would not be befitting for the Creator, who is One, to legislate many contradictory truths, religions and ways, and be an author of confusion. Consequently, Allaah forbade mankind from following anything other than the one way that He has ordained for them, saying: **"And follow not other ways."** The wisdom behind staying away from other paths is clear, as the remaining part of this verse clarifies: **"For they will separate you away from His Way."**

Believing that the Creator ordained many contradictory ways to worship and obey Him does not make logical sense. This belief entails that the Creator created and sustains everything with absolute wisdom, yet failed to outline a complete path which He wills His creation to follow. It would go against the wisdom of the Creator to ordain many ways, because pluralism causes people's concepts of good and bad to become unclear. Pluralism also causes people's understanding of who the Creator is and what He wants from His creation to become obscured.

Likewise, under these pluralistic circumstances, people's rights become squandered, as no set system of values exists which would be able to guarantee people certain basic, irrevocable rights. As a result of this approach to life, all beliefs and values become subject to change at any time.

In short, pluralism breeds confusion and contradiction in the most basic matters of life, and causes mankind to be divided. Division of thought and ideology causes splitting and disputing, even if it might appear that these people are united and tolerating each other's different ways.

For this reason, the Creator described the condition of those who would differ in fundamental matters of life after having clarified His guidance in these regards as having failed to use their God-given sense of reasoning correctly:

﴿ تَحْسَبُهُمْ جَمِيعًا وَقُلُوبُهُمْ شَتَّىٰ ذَٰلِكَ بِأَنَّهُمْ قَوْمٌ لَّا يَعْقِلُونَ ﴾

You would think they are united, but their hearts are divided. That is because they are a people who understand not.
[59:14]

An Inability to Comprehend Our Purpose of Existence

In materialist and pluralist societies, people are kept busy with all kinds of different endeavours, whether they be work or entertainment related. Although the media and academia in these societies are responsible for communicating a large amount of information to the people, they leave people in the dark as to why we are actually here in this life. What could possibly be more important than knowing about the purpose of life?

Many materialists and pluralists today still believe in the existence of a Creator. After affirming the creational aspect of God's oneness, many of these same people claim that no one particular truth exists, or that nobody should claim that they follow absolute truth from their Creator. This belief directly implies that the God who created them did so for no particular reason, and that nobody should claim that there is any one specific purpose to life.

﴿ أَفَحَسِبْتُمْ أَنَّمَا خَلَقْنَاكُمْ عَبَثًا وَأَنَّكُمْ إِلَيْنَا لَا تُرْجَعُونَ ١١٥ ﴾

Did you then think that We had created you in jest (without any purpose), and that you would not be brought back to Us (for account)?
[23:115]

Belief in the existence of an All-Knowing and All-Wise Creator necessitates that He created us for a very important reason:

﴿ وَمَا خَلَقْتُ ٱلْجِنَّ وَٱلْإِنسَ إِلَّا لِيَعْبُدُونِ ﴾

I have not created the Jinn and mankind except to worship and serve Me (alone).
[51:56]

If mankind was created to worship and serve the Creator, certainly, He would have explained to His creation how this should be done.[19] However, many people today believe that Allaah neglected sending down one perfect religion and way of life that is pleasing to Him. They claim that the ways to God are many, and that it is up to the individual to make up his or her own "personal path to God." Since they do not believe that their Creator ordained one set path for them to follow, they also conclude that mankind is not answerable to Him regarding whether or not they followed this one way.

Interestingly enough, if one of these people were to buy something mundane like a piece of unassembled furniture and found that there was no assembly guide in the box, he or she would almost certainly return to the store it was bought from and demand one. Amazingly, people expect to receive a reference guide for their material goods, but do not expect any guideline to be sent down from their Creator in regards to their worship, lives and ultimate destiny.

Indeed, they believe that God exists, yet at the same time, they disbelieve that He sends down absolute guidance to them as to how they should

[19] The Creator ordered his final Messenger (ﷺ) to convey His legislation to mankind, promising to protect this final revelation from any form of corruption:

﴿ إِنَّا نَحْنُ نَزَّلْنَا ٱلذِّكْرَ وَإِنَّا لَهُۥ لَحَٰفِظُونَ ﴾

We have, without doubt, sent down the *Qur'aan*; and We will assuredly guard it (from corruption).
[15:9]

Amazingly, to this day, Muslims all over the world read exactly the same *Qur'aan*, which has not been changed with time, unlike the former, abrogated scriptures.

relate to Him and the rest of the creation. This is not a belief that is limited to modernity. On the contrary, it is a belief that has already been mentioned in the *Qur'aan* over 1,400 years ago:

﴿ وَمَا قَدَرُوا۟ ٱللَّهَ حَقَّ قَدْرِهِۦٓ إِذْ قَالُوا۟ مَآ أَنزَلَ ٱللَّهُ عَلَىٰ بَشَرٍ مِّن شَىْءٍ ﴾

No just estimate of Allaah did they make when they said: "Nothing did Allaah send down to any human being (by revelation)."
[6:91]

A Cause for Disorientation, Discord and Discontent

Denying that Allaah sends down guidance to His creation causes people to be confused and misguided, as besides their Creator, there is none to guide them if He does not will guidance for them. The final prophet sent to mankind expressed this in the following way:

"Whomever Allaah guides, none can lead astray,
and whomever Allaah leads astray, [20] *none can guide."*[21]

The confusion and misguidance which comes about from the illogical conviction of believing in the existence of God,[22] while denying that He

[20] Allaah does not misguide anyone until they themselves turn away from His Signs. Allaah's Signs are found both within the creation and within His revelation. Each of these types of Signs point to the fact that none has created mankind except Him alone, and that as such, nothing deserves to be worshipped and served, except Him alone.

[21] Related by Muslim (no.867)

[22] In Islaam, it is not sufficient that a person say "I believe in God," meaning only in reality, "I believe in the *existence* of God." On April 24, 2000, Richard Morin of *The Washington Post* wrote an article entitled "Do Americans Believe in God?" Confirming that the meaning of the title "believe in God" solely means, "believe in the *existence* of God," Morin writes: "What's more, belief in God may be getting stronger. In 1987, a Gallup poll found that 60 percent of those interviewed "completely agreed" with the statement, "I never doubt the **existence** of God."

Those people who claim that they "believe in God," while in reality, only believe that God exists, failed to actually implement their faith in the existence of God by sincerely singling Him out in all worship and obedience. Believing in the existence of God necessitates acting upon this belief with correct and sincere action.

sent down guidance to His creation, can be witnessed in the contradictory statements of its adherents. In the previously mentioned poll that quotes 92% of Americans believing in the existence of God, the same poll shows that only 85% of these people believe in heaven. Perhaps upon the basis of "thinking positively," only 74% of those polled said they believed in the existence of hell. These numbers differed drastically, according to the age of those polled, with each segment of society claiming different things about their Lord and His religion: "An 86 percent majority of adults between the ages of 18 to 34 believe in hell, but that drops to 68 percent for those over age 70."[23]

In an article tellingly entitled "Most believe in heaven and think they'll go there," *The Los Angeles Times'* Connie Kang reported that an overwhelming majority of Americans "continue to believe there is life after death and that heaven and hell exist, according to a new study. What's more, most think they are heaven-bound."

Speaking about this majority, Kang said: "**Nearly two-thirds** of Americans in the national survey said that they believe they will go to heaven. **Only one half of 1 percent** said they were hell-bound." Regarding this finding, Kang quotes theologian Robert Johnston, a professor of theology and culture at Fuller Theological Seminary in Pasadena, California, as saying: "We're optimists at heart. If you really believe in hell, you wouldn't want to be there."

The fact that nearly two-thirds of Americans "believe they will go to heaven" and "only one half of 1 percent said they were hell-bound" shows that these people who have been surveyed have created a false sense of security for themselves.

﴿ أَفَأَمِنُوا۟ مَكْرَ ٱللَّهِ ۚ فَلَا يَأْمَنُ مَكْرَ ٱللَّهِ إِلَّا ٱلْقَوْمُ ٱلْخَـٰسِرُونَ ﴿٩٩﴾ ﴾

Did they then feel secure against the Plan of Allaah? For none feels secure from the Plan of Allaah, except those who are doomed to ruin.
[7:99]

Allaah alone decides who will be admitted into heaven, and who will be punished in hell. Saying otherwise entails speaking about the Creator without insight or authority from Him:

---

[23] Dana Blanton, More Believe In God Than Heaven, *FOX News*, October 16, 2003.

﴿ وَلَا تَقْفُ مَا لَيْسَ لَكَ بِهِۦ عِلْمٌ ۚ إِنَّ ٱلسَّمْعَ وَٱلْبَصَرَ وَٱلْفُؤَادَ كُلُّ أُو۟لَٰٓئِكَ كَانَ عَنْهُ مَسْـُٔولًا ﴿٣٦﴾ ﴾

And follow not (O man), that of which you have no knowledge. Verily, the hearing, the sight, and the heart; each of those will be questioned (by Allaah).
[17:36]

According to the texts of the *Qur'aan* and *Sunnah*,[24] a true believer in God should relate to Him with both fear and hope. Instead of believing he or she "will go to heaven" or is "hell-bound," the believer should worship Allaah with fear of Him, and with hope that His boundless mercy will envelop them. Having true love of Allaah necessitates achieving this balance. This balance can only be implemented after the believer strives to worship and obey Allaah as He wills to be worshipped and obeyed, according to His ordained way. Anything short of this sincere effort entails self-deception.

Cutting and Pasting Religious Views

Describing the problem that arises when treating religion in a democratic manner, Kang quotes David Kinnaman, the vice president of the research group which carried out the poll, as saying: "Millions of Americans mix secular and various religious views to create their personal belief systems." Unabashedly, Kinnaman says: "Americans don't mind embracing contradictions... It's hyper-individualism. They're cutting and pasting religious views from a variety of different sources - television, movies, [and] conversations with their friends."

Explaining how people are able to invent a religion by themselves, Kinnaman states: "What Americans are saying is, 'Listen, I can probably put together a philosophy of life for myself that is just as accurate, just as helpful as any particular faith might provide.'"[25]

[24] The *Sunnah* comprises the sayings, actions and approvals of the Prophet Muhammad (ﷺ), the final Messenger sent to mankind.

[25] K. Connie Kang, Most believe in heaven and think they'll go there, *Los Angeles Times*, October 25, 2003.

Amazingly, many people believe that God knows everything, yet still proceed to put together a philosophy, religion, or way of life for themselves. Certainly, this belief necessitates that this All-Knowing God has created us without ordaining a way of life for us, or that He has, but that mankind can put together their own way of life that is superior to His.

The notion of each individual creating their own "personal" belief system by "cutting and pasting" "secular and various religious views" together from "television, movies," and "conversations with their friends," is not something limited to popular American thought. On the contrary, many people are presently living by this convenient reality.

All of these convictions come about from the kind of chaos that Thomas Friedman invited his readers to believe in, when he stated that God "welcomes different human beings approaching him through their own history, out of their language and cultural heritage."[26] Furthermore, the principle that David Kinnaman mentions, namely, "Listen, I can probably put together a philosophy of life for myself that is just as accurate, just as helpful as any particular faith might provide" confirms that Allaah is certainly aware of what His creation is doing, when He says:

﴿ إِن يَتَّبِعُونَ إِلَّا ٱلظَّنَّ وَمَا تَهْوَى ٱلْأَنفُسُ ۖ وَلَقَدْ جَآءَهُم مِّن رَّبِّهِمُ ٱلْهُدَىٰٓ ﴾

They follow nothing but conjecture and what their own souls desire, even though there has already come to them Guidance from their Lord. [53:23]

Creating Moral Anarchy

Expressed in another way, the belief that Thomas Friedman and many other people hold today - namely that there are many paths that lead to God - can be refuted in the following manner: If somebody came to rob Friedman's home, he would certainly object to this occurring. Were he to have the opportunity to speak to the robber and scold him for his action, Friedman would certainly be taken aback if the robber suddenly told him that there was nothing wrong in taking his belongings. It could be argued by the robber that each person has the right to choose

[26] Thomas L. Friedman, The Real War, *New York Times*, November 27, 2001.

their own path in life, and that it is part of his own system of belief which he has formulated for himself that there is nothing wrong with stealing.

Under this pluralistic pretext, the robber would be able to tell Friedman that he tolerates Friedman's belief that nobody should steal his things, but that Friedman should also understand that he has his own personal way which he has formulated that does not consider this action to be a crime. This approach to morals and beliefs **necessitates that no absolute truth exists**, and as such, **it is not possible for anybody to impose their opinion on anyone else**, as **no clear criterion exists to justify this**. Just as Friedman would object to this kind of moral anarchy taking place amongst his society, how can he be pleased to relegate this kind of philosophical chaos to an All-Knowing, All-Wise God?

A Conclusive Proof

Surely, the incredible unity and order that exists from one end of the universe to the other indicates that the Creator's creational will within His creation is a single will, not multiple ones with each section of the universe having separate truths, laws and ways. Likewise, the Creator's will on matters related to our lives and worship is one of unity and order, not disorder with each incredibly limited individual being left to figure out their own truths and ways. Had Allaah allowed His creation to be subjected to what Friedman has referred to, the whole universe would cease being a place of unity and order, and would become a place of turmoil and disruption.

﴿ وَلَوِ ٱتَّبَعَ ٱلْحَقُّ أَهْوَآءَهُمْ لَفَسَدَتِ ٱلسَّمَـٰوَٰتُ وَٱلْأَرْضُ وَمَن فِيهِنَّ ۚ بَلْ أَتَيْنَـٰهُم بِذِكْرِهِمْ فَهُمْ عَن ذِكْرِهِم مُّعْرِضُونَ ﴿٧١﴾ ﴾

"And if the truth had been in accordance with their desires, truly, the heavens and the earth, and all beings therein would have been in a state of confusion and corruption. Nay, We have brought them their admonition, but they turn away from their reminder."
[23:71]

How Does Islaam Enlighten People?

The Contributions of Islaamic Civilization

In a notorious *Sunday Express* article boldly entitled "We owe the Arabs nothing," British columnist Robert Kilroy-Silk made the following statement: "Apart from oil - which was discovered, is produced and is paid for paid for by the west - what do they contribute? Can you think of anything? Anything really useful? Anything really valuable? Something we really need, could not do without? No, nor can I." [27]

When expressing himself, Kilroy-Silk seems oblivious of the fact that many of the sciences and forms of scholarship Westerners now excel in were passed on to them by the Arabs and Muslims. Kilroy-Silk could consider the contributions Muslims made to academic enquiry, science, geometry, astronomy, mathematics, algebra (an Arabic word), chemistry, geography, engineering, history, law, medicine, pharmacology, hygiene, etiquette, optics, architecture, agriculture and open trade, as well as the creation of hospitals, expansive libraries and universities.[28]

---

[27] Brian Whitaker, Kilroy-Silk investigated for anti-Arab comments, *The Guardian*, January 8, 2004.

[28] After explaining that Muslims are "commanded by the Koran to seek knowledge and read nature for signs of the Creator," Dennis Overbye, *The New York Times'* science columnist, had the following to say: "Muslims created a society that in the Middle Ages was the scientific center of the world. The Arabic language was synonymous with learning and science for 500 hundred years, a golden age that can count among its credits the precursors to modern universities, algebra, the names of the stars and even the notion of science as an empirical inquiry.

'Nothing in Europe could hold a candle to what was going on in the Islamic world until about 1600,' said Dr. Jamil Ragep, a professor of the history of science at the University of Oklahoma.

It was the infusion of this knowledge into Western Europe, historians say, that fueled the Renaissance and the scientific revolution."

=

The late scholar of Islaam, Shaykh 'Abdur-Rahmaan as-Sa'dee (d.1956, 1376H), clarified how the earlier generations of Muslims successfully "established their fields of knowledge, perceptions, faith and deeds upon true, **firmly established fundamentals**. These fundamentals are the heavenly revealed books, the guidance of the prophets, Allaah's Signs within mankind and the universe, and sound intellects. Due to the following of these fundamentals, they succeeded with good in this world and the hereafter."[29]

Although the West has certainly excelled in many areas of knowledge, they have also severely restricted their fields of knowledge by overlooking the firmly established fundamentals as-Sa'dee has mentioned above.

Humanism: The Cause of Straying in Western Thought and Belief

One of the problems with Western scholasticism is that it relies solely upon human intellect, even though rational people are aware of the fact that human understanding alone is very limited in scope. It can be observed that human understanding is constantly changing, relying upon the established thoughts of a particular era. As such, humanist thought cannot isolate mankind's long-term goals, needs and interests, as humanism relies solely upon the intellect of human beings, which is in reality, tremendously limited.

﴿ وَمَآ أُوتِيتُم مِّنَ ٱلْعِلْمِ إِلَّا قَلِيلًا ﴾

Overbye quotes Dr. David King, a historian of science at Johann Wolfgang Goethe University in Frankfurt, as saying: "Why did Muslim science decline?" he said. "That's a very Western question. **It flourished for a thousand years - no civilization on Earth has flourished that long in that way.**"

Regarding the decline of the Islaamic golden age of scientific discovery, Overbye said: "Humiliating encounters with Western colonial powers in the 19th century produced a hunger for Western science and technology, or at least the economic and military power they could produce, scholars say. Reformers bent on modernizing Eastern educational systems to include Western science could argue that Muslims would only be reclaiming their own, since the West had inherited science from the Islamic world to begin with." (How Islam Won, and Lost, the Lead in Science, Dennis Overbye, *The New York Times*, October 30, 2001.)

[29] Shaykh 'Abdur-Rahmaan as-Sa'dee, *al-Adillatul-Qawaati' wal-Baraaheen fee Ibtaal Usool-il-Mulhideen*, *Daarul-Minhaaj*, p.88.

"And of knowledge, you have been given only a little."
[17:85]

Although Western society has formed an economic and political system upon which it prides itself, it does not prepare people for the day they will die and meet their Creator. Not only does humanist thought fail to prepare people for their everlasting and more important existence, it does not even succeed in helping them understand why they are here in this life.

﴿ يَعْلَمُونَ ظَـٰهِرًا مِّنَ ٱلْحَيَوٰةِ ٱلدُّنْيَا وَهُمْ عَنِ ٱلْـَٔاخِرَةِ هُمْ غَـٰفِلُونَ ۝٧ ﴾

They know only the outer (things) of the life of this world; but of the Hereafter, they are heedless.
[30:7]

The acquisition of true knowledge normally leads to humility when approached in a sincere manner. One who acquires true knowledge realizes how little they really know. However, when it is approached in a materialistically restricted manner, it causes people to become proud. This flawed approach to seeking knowledge is not something new, and has precedents from others who have lived in former ages:

﴿ فَلَمَّا جَآءَتْهُمْ رُسُلُهُم بِٱلْبَيِّنَـٰتِ فَرِحُوا۟ بِمَا عِندَهُم مِّنَ ٱلْعِلْمِ ۝٨٣ ﴾

Then when their Messengers came to them with clear proofs, they exulted in the knowledge (of worldly things) that they had.
[40:83]

When considering these matters, as-Sa'dee explains how it becomes evident that "mankind is imperfect in nature from every perspective, and that whatever they have in the way of knowledge and capability is due to Allaah having given them this knowledge and capability. It should also be considered that Allaah appointed a limit to mankind's knowledge and capability which cannot be extended... Just as Allaah is the One who created them when they were not even a thing mentioned, He is also the One who made them come out from their mothers' wombs knowing nothing, and created for them the ability to hear, see and understand, and the means to acquire knowledge."[30]

[30] Ibid, p.55.

Humanism's restricted approach to seeking knowledge has made mankind forgetful that every single piece of information that any human being has ever perceived came from an All-Knowing Creator:

﴿ قَالُوا۟ سُبْحَـٰنَكَ لَا عِلْمَ لَنَآ إِلَّا مَا عَلَّمْتَنَآ ۖ إِنَّكَ أَنتَ ٱلْعَلِيمُ ٱلْحَكِيمُ ﴿٣٢﴾ ﴾

They (angels) said: "Glory be unto You; we have no knowledge except what You have taught us. Verily, you are the All-Knower, the All-Wise."
[2:32]

A Forgetful and Unbalanced Approach to Science

Notes as-Sa'dee: "One of the greatest forms of betrayal to knowledge and reality (that occurs) is the severing of all connection to Allaah and His religion that scientists make when undertaking research. For verily, they make countless investigations into the various forms of creation, and from their inquiries, they derive many benefits. However, along with that, we do not find them mentioning God in any of these investigations, nor do they estimate the Creator and Arranger of these creations with a just estimation when undergoing these investigations. Furthermore, they do not give any kind of thanks to the One who has bestowed the creation with countless favours, nor do they mention His will and capability in bringing about what He wants within the creation. This occurs to such an extent that those who doubt, rather, many from the researchers themselves, deem that these various forms of creation which they are investigating are all that exist, and that there is no existence beyond them. Hence, they fall into open denial (of the Creator and His capabilities), and thus become confounded when it comes to adhering to correct belief:

﴿ بَلْ كَذَّبُوا۟ بِٱلْحَقِّ لَمَّا جَآءَهُمْ فَهُمْ فِىٓ أَمْرٍ مَّرِيجٍ ﴿٥﴾ ﴾

Nay, but they have denied the truth[31] when it has come to them, so they are in a state of confusion.
[50:5]

If only they had established what was required of them and upon the rest of mankind in the way of founding their information upon their true

[31] Meaning: The *Qur'aan* and the knowledge it contains

realities and fundamentals, attributing the existence of the creation to their Originator, and attributing the favours (they witness within the creation) to the One who conferred them, they would have been guided to a straight way (in their worldly and religious affairs)."[32]

An Imbalance That Leads to a State of Confusion

Having overlooked the firmly established fundamentals that were mentioned in the beginning of the book,[33] materialist scholars are still searching for true understanding and insight into some of the most crucial issues that face mankind. As-Sa'dee addressed these scholars, saying: "You are still engaged in the fields of knowledge that you pride yourselves in, and are still inventing theories that you all agree upon, or (at least) most of them, and you form final decisions regarding them, you believe in them, and you authoritatively assert their truthfulness. Then after your repeated reflection and consideration regarding these theories, you begin to doubt them, and perhaps you (now) authoritatively assert their falsehood, and proceed to invent that which contradicts them with (new) theories...

And how many theories do you deny that you once deemed to be true? This is the reality and outcome of your higher fields of knowledge. How then, can someone who possesses the lowest level of intellect, allow these theories to oppose that which the messengers came with in the way of truthful information?"[34]

How Islaam Encouraged Nations of People to Acquire Knowledge For Over a Millennium

Furthermore, states as-Sa'dee, "the heads and scholars of the atheists [and those who agree with some of the fundamentals of atheism] are still devoted to finding solutions to different crisis that face us in life through their various efforts and sciences. In reality, they have fallen short in every way imaginable in trying to fulfill this. For every time they find a solution to a problem, numerous problems arise from this solution...

---

[32] Shaykh 'Abdur-Rahmaan as-Sa'dee, op. cit., p.42-43.

[33] The first three chapters have dealt with the subjects of the existence of a Creator, why He alone deserves to be worshipped and served in our lives, and how He has sent down revelation which shows us how this worship and servitude should be carried out.

[34] Ibid, p.29.

An example of the problems that have caused great disorder and confusion for mankind... is that of knowledge... For if it is sound, all of the different beliefs and ways of thinking will also be sound, and the actions that are founded upon it will be correct. Indeed, the legislated law and way of life of Islaam exhorts people to seek knowledge, **awakening in them a strong desire to do so**. And it commands mankind to learn all of the various beneficial fields of knowledge, whether they be from the worldly or religious affairs...

As for the fields of knowledge related to religion, the legislated law and way of life of Islaam has detailed these fields of knowledge to the utmost, after having laid out their fundamentals. As for the fields of knowledge related to worldly matters, the legislated law and way of life of Islaam has laid out the foundation for their fundamentals and principles, and guides mankind to them...

As for the materialists, they only consider knowledge to be the fields of knowledge that are related to worldly affairs, which are (in reality) only a means of arriving at greater ends. Furthermore, they malign and disparage the fields of knowledge related to religion, (even though) their sciences do not in actuality benefit mankind unless they be used along with these fields of religious knowledge... For this reason, their fields of knowledge have become unsettled, and they have found themselves to be in a state of confusion, contradicting themselves with their conflicting views and unstable philosophies.

Another problem that faces mankind is that of wealth and poverty: It has already preceded that this religion and way of life provides solutions that perfect mankind's affairs in which they experience a pleasant life of content. Just as this religion and way of life commands people to obtain a livelihood through permissible ways that are appropriate for every time and place, it has also commanded mankind to seek Allaah's aid in obtaining this livelihood, and to avoid the impermissible ways [that eventually harm them] when obtaining it. In short, Islaam has directed mankind to fulfill what is incumbent upon them in acquiring the various forms of necessary wealth.

Likewise, Islaam has commanded mankind to be patient during the advent of poverty, and to face that with submission and not to be discontent with what has been written for them, while striving hard to obtain sustenance through the various forms of work and income. It has also **for-**

bidden mankind to be idle or lazy, which harms them in their religious and worldly affairs."[35]

Prophet Muhammad (ﷺ) used to say: "O *Allaah! I seek refuge in you from laziness.*"[36] Likewise, he also explained to his companions the following principle which, when implemented, led nations and civilizations to greatness: "*Strive for what benefits you, seek the help of Allaah, and do not be lazy or incapable.*"[37]

A Prevailing Doubt in the World Today: "Look at the State of Affairs of the Muslims!"

In reference to one of the major contentions that materialist thinkers spread today, as-Sa'dee comments: "They say: 'Look at the state of affairs of the Muslims and how weak they are;' that they are lagging behind in their worldly affairs, and that the thing which held them back is their religion; they propagate this in many different ways." As-Sa'dee replies that it would have been more befitting for those who deem this to be true to examine the religion of Islaam in itself, and "what it possesses in the way of exactitude, excellence and perfection, and what it possesses in the way of guidance to every kind of good, and protection from every kind of harm and evil."

"Furthermore," he says, "it is also incumbent to look at the state of those who are implementing its tenets and rulings within themselves and between the people, as it was being implemented at the dawn of Islaam.[38] For whoever does so will find that which delights its onlookers, and that which establishes the proof upon the obstinate. As for the scrutinizing of the Muslims who have strayed (from its straight way) by having abandoned its guidance, directives and lofty tenets, that is surely a form of injustice."[39]

---

[35] Ibid, p.46-47.

[36] Reported by al-Bukhaaree (no. 6371)

[37] Related by Muslim (no. 2664)

[38] The Prophet (ﷺ) directed the Muslims to understand and implement Islaam according to "*that which I and my Companions are upon.*" (Authenticated by Shaykh al-Albaanee in *Saheeh Sunan at-Tirmidhee* (3/54)) Likewise, he (ﷺ) also said, "*The best of mankind is my generation, then those who follow them, then those who follow them.*" (Related by al-Bukhaaree (no. 2652))

[39] Shaykh 'Abdur-Rahmaan as-Sa'dee, op. cit, p.60.

A Return to a Balanced Approach in Acquiring Knowledge

All happiness and success begins and ends with realizations that do not contradict true knowledge that has been revealed by the Creator. The ill effects of knowledge that is based solely upon materialist ideologies are already in progress and are observable for all to see. As-Sa'dee explains that the restricting of knowledge to materialist sciences and the instability of thought and morals which has resulted from this has occurred, "because they deny true, beneficial knowledge that purifies the soul and grants it happiness, and advances it to the ways of excellence."[40]

﴿ وَجَعَلْنَا لَهُمْ سَمْعًا وَأَبْصَارًا وَأَفْئِدَةً فَمَآ أَغْنَىٰ عَنْهُمْ سَمْعُهُمْ وَلَآ أَبْصَارُهُمْ وَلَآ
أَفْئِدَتُهُم مِّن شَىْءٍ إِذْ كَانُوا۟ يَجْحَدُونَ بِـَٔايَٰتِ ٱللَّهِ
وَحَاقَ بِهِم مَّا كَانُوا۟ بِهِۦ يَسْتَهْزِءُونَ ﴾

And We had assigned them hearing, sight and hearts (understanding);
but of no profit to them were their hearing, sight and hearts,
since they used to deny the Signs of Allaah;
and they were completely encircled by
that which they used to mock at.
[46:26]

In the end, the fields of knowledge that mankind has now excelled in will not profit them until they found them upon the firmly established fundamentals that have been mentioned in the first part of this book.[41] The likeness of affirming only the subsidiary branches of knowledge such as those things related to material findings, while denying the fundamental issues of knowledge found within authentic revelation from the Creator, is like building a beautiful palace while forgetting to lay its foundations. In the end, it is destined to crumble.

---

[40] Ibid, p.20.

[41] The first three chapters have dealt with the subjects of the existence of a Creator, why He alone deserves to be worshipped and served in our lives, and how He has sent down revelation which shows us how this worship and servitude should be carried out.

﴿ أَفَمَنْ أَسَّسَ بُنْيَـٰنَهُۥ عَلَىٰ تَقْوَىٰ مِنَ ٱللَّهِ وَرِضْوَٰنٍ خَيْرٌ أَم مَّنْ أَسَّسَ بُنْيَـٰنَهُۥ عَلَىٰ شَفَا جُرُفٍ هَارٍ ﴾

"Is then he who laid the foundation of his building on piety to Allaah and His Good Pleasure better, or he who laid the foundation of his building on the brink of an undetermined precipice, ready to crumble down..."
[9:109]

Is Islaam a Regressive Religion and Way of Life?

The True Causes of Decline

On September 26, 2001, Italian Prime Minister Silvio Berlusconi openly declared to a group of reporters that Islaamic civilization is "stuck where it was 1,400 years ago."[42]

Berlusconi's belief that Islaamic civilization is "stuck where it was 1,400 years ago" is an inaccurate assessment, both from a religious and historical perspective. From a religious perspective, a great number of Muslims in today's world are far removed from the guidance that is contained within the *Qur'aan* and *Sunnah*, the two sources of revelation that were revealed over 1,400 years ago. For example, through the occupation of Iraq, Westerners have been exposed to the so-called "holy cities" of Kufa, Karbala and Najaf, in which the *Shee'ah* hover around graves of their dead religious leaders, worshipping them with great humility and fanfare. This occurs, even though it is known that the *Qur'aan* and *Sunnah* only affirm the special status of Makkah, Madeenah and Jerusalem. Furthermore, the *Qur'aan* and *Sunnah* specifically censure any form of false worship, including the worship of graves.[43]

Many of those who are presently claiming to be *Sunnee*[44] are also far removed from the clarity that is contained within the *Qur'aan* and *Sunnah*. Over the passage of time, they have fallen into the blind following of their

---

[42] Berlusconi: The West must conquer Islam, *Associated Press: Salon*, September 26, 2001.

[43] The Prophet Muhammad (ﷺ) said: "*Those who came before you took the graves of their prophets and pious people as places of worship. Do not take the graves as places of worship, for verily, I forbid you to do so.*" Related by Muslim (no. 1188).

[44] The word *Sunnee* is derived from the word *Sunnah*. The *Sunnah* comprises the sayings, actions and approvals of the Prophet (ﷺ). The Prophet (ﷺ) said: "*He who turns away from my Sunnah is not from me.*" (Reported by al-Bukhaaree (no. 5063))

forefathers and have thus acquired certain beliefs, superstitions and rites of worship that have no basis in the religion of Islaam. Others have split up the Muslim nation into groups, sects and parties, with each group either falling into forms of extremism or negligence. In short, a great portion of the Muslims have become far removed from implementing Islaam as it should be implemented, in belief, speech, and action.

For this reason, the Creator is not pleased with Muslims who do not adhere carefully to His revelation, and sends down trials upon them out of His justice and mercy, perchance they may take heed.

﴿ ظَهَرَ ٱلْفَسَادُ فِى ٱلْبَرِّ وَٱلْبَحْرِ بِمَا كَسَبَتْ أَيْدِى ٱلنَّاسِ

لِيُذِيقَهُم بَعْضَ ٱلَّذِى عَمِلُوا۟ لَعَلَّهُمْ يَرْجِعُونَ ﴿٤١﴾ ﴾

Evil has appeared on land and sea, because of what the hands of men have earned. That Allaah may make them taste a part of that which they have done, in order that they may return (to Him) in repentance.

[30:41]

Contrary to what Berlusconi would have people believe, the Muslims will only find relief from the calamities they are facing when they return to their religion in the manner that their Creator has ordained for them. They will not find true relief in distancing themselves from His chosen way.

﴿ وَبَلَوْنَٰهُم بِٱلْحَسَنَٰتِ وَٱلسَّيِّـَٔاتِ لَعَلَّهُمْ يَرْجِعُونَ ﴾

And We tested them with good blessings and evil calamities, in order that they may return (to the obedience of Allaah).

[7:168]

Berlusconi believes that Islaamic civilization is "stuck where it was 1,400 years ago." However, had it really been true that the Muslims were stuck doing what the Prophet Muhammad (ﷺ) and his Companions were doing over 1,400 years ago in the way of creed, morals and manners, Allaah would have opened up every kind of worldly good for them. This is what Islaamic civilization had already experienced off and on for over a millennium. Adhering to the original understanding of Islaam from over 1,400 years ago is textually corroborated by the saying of the final Prophet (ﷺ),

who described the acceptable understanding of Islaam as being "*that which I and my Companions are upon.*"[45]

﴿ فَإِنْ ءَامَنُوا۟ بِمِثْلِ مَآ ءَامَنتُم بِهِۦ فَقَدِ ٱهْتَدَوا۟ ﴾

"**So if they believe as you** (i.e. the Prophet (ﷺ) and his Companions) **believe, they are indeed rightly guided.**"
[2:137]

Just as it cannot be said that Islaamic civilization is "stuck where it was 1,400 years ago" from a religious perspective, neither can the worldly decline Muslims face today be dated back 1,400 years. To say so would imply that the religion of Islaam impeded Muslim civilization ever since its inception over 1,400 years ago, which is exactly what Berlusconi would like to have people believe. However, would it be possible to believe that the Creator would ordain a way that hinders His creation from achieving true success?

﴿ يَظُنُّونَ بِٱللَّهِ غَيْرَ ٱلْحَقِّ ظَنَّ ٱلْجَٰهِلِيَّةِ ﴾

They hold false thoughts of Allaah - thoughts of ignorance.
[3:154]

Not only is it a logical impossibility to believe that an All-Knowing Creator would ordain a way that hinders His creation, history proves that the Muslims only benefited in their worldly affairs when they adhered to their religion.

The Flowering of a Great Civilization

Even critics of Islaam such as Bernard Lewis concede that from a worldly perspective, Islaamic civilization was a great force to be reckoned with for over a millennium, and that the decline of this civilization has only occurred within the last three centuries:

"In the period which European historians see as a dark interlude between the decline of ancient civilization - Greece and Rome - and the rise of modern civilization - Europe," states Lewis, "**Islam was the leading civilization in the world**, marked as such by its great and powerful kingdoms, its rich and varied industry and commerce, its original and creative sciences and letters."

---

[45] Authenticated by Shaykh al-Albaanee in *Saheeh Sunan at-Tirmidhee* (3/54).

"Islam, far more than Christendom," adds Lewis, "was the intermediate stage between the ancient East and the modern West, to which it contributed significantly."

However, notes Lewis, "**during the past <u>three centuries</u>**, the Islamic world has lost its dominance and its leadership, and has fallen behind both the modern West and the rapidly modernizing Orient."[46]

Leaving Off the Correct Practice of Islaam: A Historical Turning Point

An important link can be made between significant numbers of Muslims neglecting the guidance contained within the *Qur'aan* and *Sunnah*, and thus waning religiously, and the eventual decline of Islaamic civilization. Both of these matters occurred on a larger scale within the past few hundred years, not 1,400 years ago. It can therefore be concluded that the moral and religious lapse that became compounded in the last few centuries also caused Muslim societies to fall into material decline.

When the Muslims were following the guidance contained in the *Qur'aan* and *Sunnah* with regards to beliefs, morals, worship, politics and interpersonal dealings, their Sustainer was pleased with them and provided them with every kind of success. However, when many of them turned away from this guidance, the Controller of all affairs became displeased with them and removed His favour from them.

The elimination of these tribulations will not occur until the Muslims themselves sincerely turn to their Creator and set their sights on the way that carried them so effectively for over a millennium - until many of them abandoned it and turned towards other ways that were founded upon conjecture and uncertainty.

﴿ إِنَّ ٱللَّهَ لَا يُغَيِّرُ مَا بِقَوْمٍ حَتَّىٰ يُغَيِّرُوا۟ مَا بِأَنفُسِهِمْ ﴾

Verily, Allaah will not change the situation of a people until they change their own condition.
[13:11]

[46] Bernard Lewis, The Crisis of Islam, *The New York Times*, April 6, 2003.

Indeed, the Prophet (ﷺ) warned the Muslims about the dire results of disobeying the Creator and turning away from His guidance. Addressing them, he (ﷺ) said: *"Allaah will send humiliation upon you and will not remove it until you* ***return to your religion****."*[47]

This connection between neglect in religion and societal decline is a historical fact that cannot be denied by anyone who has studied Islaamic civilization. Furthermore, it is a point that completely nullifies the prejudiced claim that Islaamic civilization is somehow "stuck where it was 1,400 years ago," as Berlusconi has conveniently overlooked the fact that Islaamic civilization flourished for over one thousand years.

Muslims will once again be able to experience this kind of success when they sincerely return to the timeless guidance that granted them success for such an extended period of time. Although our materialist societies might teach us to sneer at such types of statements, many of those who would mock such beliefs actually also affirm the existence of a Creator. Once they have affirmed the existence of a Creator, they are obliged to admit that ultimately, He alone owns everything within the heavens and the earth. Once this has been established, it also becomes apparent that He alone controls the affairs of His creation, including those affairs that affect His servants. Hence, in the end, it is correct to believe that everything that occurs to human societies occurs by His knowledge, capability and will.

After considering things from a religious and historical perspective, it becomes apparent that Prime Minister Berlusconi's statement that Islaamic civilization is "stuck where it was 1400 years ago" is not an accurate assessment of the current difficulties Muslims are experiencing. More importantly, history has proven that when Muslims adhered to Islaam, they met with success, while when they waned in their practice of Islaam, they experienced many moral, economic, and societal obstacles.

As such, it can be concluded that Islaam is not the regressive religion and way of life that Berlusconi and others claim it to be. On the contrary, true progress can only be achieved by keeping people in touch with the realities of life, not by moving from one form of human conjecture to another. This methodology causes people's morals and societal structures to deteriorate from generation to generation without them perceiving it.

---

[47] Authenticated by Shaykh al-Albaanee in *Saheeh Sunan Abee Daawood* (no. 3462).

"In February [2004], an Iraqi reporter asked Army Brig. Gen. Mark Kimmitt, spokesman for the occupation forces, what he would recommend Iraqi mothers tell their children frightened by low-flying helicopters.

'What we would tell the children of Iraq is that the noise they hear is the sound of freedom,' Kimmitt said."[48]

[48] Jim Krane, Copters Maxed in Counterinsurgency War, *The Associated Press*, November 1, 2004.

Understanding Freedom, Diversity and Tolerance

The Coerced Freedom to Accept Western Values

Speaking about freedom, diversity and tolerance, Italian Prime Minister Silvio Berlusconi openly contradicted himself while speaking about the merits of Western civilization. Addressing a group of reporters at a news conference, Berlusconi was quoted as saying: "We must be aware of the superiority of our civilization, a system that has guaranteed well-being, respect for human rights and – in contrast with Islamic countries – respect for religious and political rights, a system that has as its values understandings of diversity and tolerance."

In regards to freedom, Berlusconi claimed that Western civilization is superior, primarily because it "has at its core, as its greatest value, freedom, which is not the heritage of Islamic culture."

This concept of freedom, diversity and tolerance, consists of the freedom, diversity and tolerance to follow Western culture and values, or else be conquered - an obvious contradiction that has caused generations of nations to suffer. Said Berlusconi: "The West will continue to conquer people like it conquered Communism," even if it means a confrontation with "another civilization, the Islamic one, stuck where it was 1,400 years ago."[49]

Forming Consent to Serve an Intolerant Ideology

Some Western journalists and intellectuals have been able to perceive that liberalist ideologies are actually often intolerant by nature. After Afghanistan was attacked during the aftermath of September 11, *The Guardian's* Madeleine Bunting stated that the "public opinion formers at home have been prepared and marshalled into line with a striking degree of unanimity.

[49] Berlusconi: The West must conquer Islam, *Associated Press: Salon*, September 26, 2001.

The voices of dissent can barely be heard over the chorus of approval and self-righteous enthusiasm."

"What is also lurking here is the outline of a form of western fundamentalism," adds Bunting. "It believes in historical progress[50] and regards the west as its most advanced manifestation. And it insists that the only way for other countries to match its achievement is to adopt its political, economic and cultural values."

Discussing the concept of freedom of choice and tolerance, Bunting correctly states that like any kind of fundamentalism, Western fundamentalism "is tolerant towards other cultures **only to the extent that they reflect its own values** - so it is frequently fiercely intolerant of religious belief and has no qualms about expressing its contempt and prejudice."

"At its worst," she says, "Western fundamentalism echoes the characteristics it finds so repulsive in its enemy, Bin Laden: first, a sense of unquestioned superiority; second, an assertion of the universal applicability of its values; and third, a lack of will to understand what is profoundly different from itself."

Had the basis of Western fundamentalism been correct to begin with, its adherents could have justifiably believed in its superiority. If the term fundamentalism is used in the context of sticking closely to a set of fundamentals that can be proven to be correct, in this case, it cannot be legitimately criticized. However, if the term fundamentalism is used in the context of adhering to a set of unsubstantiated fundamentals or falling prey to fanaticism and terrorism, then it deserves to be condemned.

The Realities of Liberalism

Referring to the "shadow side of liberalism," Bunting understatedly refers to the effects of past colonialist exploits, saying that this fundamentalist ideology "periodically wreaked havoc around the globe for over 150 years."

---

[50] This belief entails that there are no absolute moral values, and that mankind can only arrive at the truth by following ever-changing opinions. The value system that transpires from this process becomes known as "human values," from which stem "human rights." However, the acceptance of these ever-changing opinions necessitates that the previous decisions and values that were made just before must have been wrong to begin with. Had it been otherwise, they would not have needed changing.

Assessing the current danger of "intolerant liberalism" and its fundamentalist belief of superiority, Bunting states: "This superiority, once allied to economic and technological power, underpinned the worst excesses of colonialism, as it now underpins the activities of multinational corporations and the IMF's[51] structural adjustment programmes."

---

[51] In a stinging October 10, 2001 article entitled "The Globalizer Who Came In From the Cold," *The Observer's* Greg Palast spoke about the injustice of the IMF/World Bank's "usurious rents" which are "devised in secrecy and driven by an absolutist ideology."

Discussing the unpleasant reality of liberalist globalisation, former World Bank Chief Economist Joseph Stiglitz spoke about the "depression and starvation" which results from "Capital Market Liberalization."

Referring to the IMF's four step program, Palast states: "Step One is Privatization - which Stiglitz said could more accurately be called, 'Briberization.'"

Step two involves a "'Hot Money' cycle," in which "cash comes in for speculation in real estate and currency, then flees at the first whiff of trouble." Palast adds, "A nation's reserves can drain in days, hours. And when that happens, to seduce speculators into returning a nation's own capital funds, the IMF demands these nations raise interest rates to 30%, 50% and 80%."

All across Asia and Latin America, the result was the same: "Higher interest rates demolished property values, savaged industrial production and drained national treasuries."

"At this point," writes Palast, "the IMF drags the gasping nation to Step Three: Market-Based Pricing, a fancy term for raising prices on food, water and cooking gas. This leads, predictably, to Step-Three-and-a-Half: what Stiglitz calls, 'The IMF riot.'"

Discussing the IMF stoked riots that have occurred in countries such as Indonesia, Bolivia and Ecuador, Palast speaks about the economic blackmail which takes place in these impoverished countries: "When a nation is, 'down and out, [the IMF] takes advantage and squeezes the last pound of blood out of them. They turn up the heat until, finally, the whole cauldron blows up,' as when the IMF eliminated food and fuel subsidies for the poor in Indonesia in 1998."

Palast claims that these tactics are part of a set IMF plan. Quoting from IMF "confidential" documents obtained by *The Observer*, Palast states that the IMF "expected their plans to spark, 'social unrest,' to use their bureaucratic term for a nation in flames."

"The secret report," says Palast, "notes that the plan to make the US dollar Ecuador's currency has pushed 51% of the population below the poverty line."

At this point of economic and social disaster, a panic occurs in which economies collapse and governments become bankrupt. It is at this point that the foreign corpora-

=

Western fundamentalism requires its adherents to believe in its "unquestioned superiority" and "the universal applicability of its values." Its adherents also lack the "will to understand what is profoundly different from itself."[52]

Something that is not willing to understand what is profoundly different from itself cannot truly be considered to be liberal, free, or part of "a system that has as its values understandings of diversity and tolerance,"[53] as Prime Minister Berlusconi would like to claim.

Once this is understood, it can be appreciated that the followers of pluralism, secularism, humanism, liberalism, freedom and democracy are also often intolerant fundamentalists, particularly if they are faced with a competing ideology that differs from theirs. Once these manmade principles are questioned, those who adhere to this fundamentalism are willing to pit nations and people together to further the cause of their belief.

﴿ وَإِذَا قِيلَ لَهُمْ لَا تُفْسِدُوا۟ فِى ٱلْأَرْضِ قَالُوٓا۟ إِنَّمَا نَحْنُ مُصْلِحُونَ ﴿١١﴾
أَلَآ إِنَّهُمْ هُمُ ٱلْمُفْسِدُونَ وَلَٰكِن لَّا يَشْعُرُونَ ﴿١٢﴾ ﴾

And when it is said to them: "Make not mischief on the earth," they say: "We are only peace-makers."

Of a surety, they are the ones who make mischief, but they perceive it not.
[2:11-12]

---

tions move in, "who can then pick off remaining assets, such as the odd mining concession or port, at fire sale prices."

Concluding, Palast asks an interesting question: "Did any nation avoid this fate? Yes, said Stiglitz, identifying Botswana. Their trick? 'They told the IMF to go packing.'"

﴿ يَٰٓأَيُّهَا ٱلَّذِينَ ءَامَنُوا۟ لَا تَأْكُلُوا۟ ٱلرِّبَوٰٓا۟ أَضْعَٰفًا مُّضَٰعَفَةً ۖ وَٱتَّقُوا۟ ٱللَّهَ لَعَلَّكُمْ تُفْلِحُونَ ﴿١٣٠﴾ ﴾

O you who believe! Do not devour usury, doubled and multiplied; but fear Allaah, that you may be successful.

[3:130]

[52] Madeleine Bunting, Intolerant liberalism, *The Guardian*, October 8, 2001.

[53] Berlusconi: The West must conquer Islam, *Associated Press: Salon*, September 26, 2001.

The Freedom to Disobey the Creator

In his comments, Berlusconi portrays the West as being a defender of freedom. However, he overlooks the fact that the West often halts people's basic freedoms of belief and expression when it comes to matters that relate to obedience to the Creator. As a Christian, Berlusconi cannot deny that wearing the veil and modesty between unmarried men and women, is both a Qur'aanic and Biblical command.[54] In fact, it is reported in the Bible that Jesus (عليه السلام) ordered his followers not to even look at women in a lustful manner: "You have heard that it was said, 'Do not commit adultery.' But I tell you that anyone who looks at a woman lustfully has already committed adultery with her in his heart."[55]

Berlusconi forgets that in Western nations, when Muslims try to apply what is actually only part of his own religion, the freedoms of belief and expression that he spoke of are often suddenly suspended. Girls who wear *hijaab* are sometimes forbidden from attending educational institutions. Women who are scantily clothed are deemed free of mind and spirit, and are allowed the freedom to dress as they like. Modest women who observe Biblical and Qur'aanic directives to veil themselves are considered oppressed, and all semblance of freedom and tolerance suddenly vanishes.

﴿ أَفَمَن كَانَ عَلَىٰ بَيِّنَةٍ مِّن رَّبِّهِۦ كَمَن زُيِّنَ لَهُۥ سُوٓءُ عَمَلِهِۦ وَٱتَّبَعُوٓاْ أَهْوَآءَهُم ﴿١٤﴾ ﴾

Is he who is on a clear proof from his Lord, like him to whom the evil of his deeds is made fairseeming, and follows his desires?
[47:14]

Although women in the West are allowed to dress as they like, they do not have absolute freedom in doing so to the point that they may walk around topless or bottomless. However, wearing just a bra-like garment with a tight mini-skirt is completely acceptable in many parts of Western society. One wonders how this distinction is made, what mankind's reference point in doing so should be, and who decides why exposing these private parts completely is a criminal offence, yet covering them slightly is a sign of liberation for women.

---

[54] The female followers of the prophets wore veils, just as practicing Muslim women do today. See: I Corinthians 11:5, Genesis 24:65, Ruth 3:15 and Isaiah 3:23.

[55] Mathew 5:27,28

A Point of Agreement

Beyond the obvious contradictions that arise from human moral legislation, it can be understood that Westerners and practicing Muslims can agree upon one thing in this case. One of the reasons why people do not accept that a woman can simply walk around naked is that it infringes on other people's rights. There is a traditional Arabic saying, which states, "*Your freedom ends when the freedom of others begins.*" What this essentially means is that an individual's freedom must be halted as soon as it starts to infringe on someone else's freedom. For that reason, Westerners feel offended if they are forced to view somebody else's private parts in a public place, just as practicing Muslims feel offended if they are forced to see someone who is scantily clad.

Hence, Muslims and Westerners both agree that freedom has its bounds, but one group holds that mankind has the right to decide in this matter, as according to them, they are free to do whatever they choose. The other side contradicts this belief, holding that the Creator is most acquainted with what is good for His creation, and that He alone has the right to decide what goes on within His dominion. Only one of these two positions can be correct.

The principle that people's freedom should be checked if it infringes on the rights of others can be observed in practice in many facets of Western society. For example, relatively new legislation has been passed in the West that curtails people's rights to smoke in public places, as this compels non-smokers to smoke, and thus infringes on other's freedoms. As a result, it is rightfully understood that this freedom must be eliminated.

Likewise, human legislation legitimately bans prostitution, as this form of sex for money has, for the meantime, been deemed immoral. Prostitution is also considered detrimental to the lives of the young women who partake in this trade. At the same time, sex for money is considered legal and acceptable, so long as it is being made into a movie for others to see. This incredible contradiction exists because banning pornography would be interpreted by contemporary minds as being an infringement of freedom and personal expression.

Ensuring Injustice and Exploitation Through Perceived Freedoms

On February 26, 2004, *The Associated Press* reported that the American House of Representatives voted "to treat attacks on a pregnant woman as separate crimes against both her and the fetus she is carrying." The bill was passed and backed by "naming it in honor of Laci and Conner Peterson, the pregnant woman who was murdered in December, 2002, and her unborn child."

The passage of the Unborn Victims of Violence act poses yet another dilemma for lawmakers and society, as it acknowledges that unborn babies do actually have rights. This admission seriously undermines the claims of pro-abortion rights activists, who claim that giving unborn children rights infringes on the rights of women to choose whether or not to kill the fetus in their wombs.

"There are two victims in these kinds of attacks," stated Rep. Melissa Hart, who was at the forefront of pushing for this new legislation. "That is so clear from the Laci and Conner Peterson case."

Unfortunately, what is so clear to some is not always clear to others. This is the quandary that faces mankind when accepting freedom of opinion in matters that the All-Knowing Creator has already legislated for mankind. In short-sightedness, some people say that Allaah's legislation is too restrictive, and that Islaam is too strict in placing barriers between men and women. This is something the Western media indoctrinates people with on a daily basis.

As it is known that all societies adhere to certain limitations, the following question needs to be asked: Is it that the Creator has mistakenly ordainned too many limitations for mankind, or that many societies fall into negligence when formulating their constantly changing system of limitations?

In truth, the Creator has legislated these limitations with full knowledge of what He brought into being, and with full knowledge of what is best for His creation. He has made avenues for mankind to enjoy sexual relations with the condition that the partners be legally conjoined, yet a portion from amongst His creation insist that it is their right to be free to have sex with whoever they want, whenever they want. Furthermore, after having practiced their perceived freedom in this matter, these individuals feel that it is from their freedom to terminate the life of what emanates from these relations, solely because the child will affect the beauty of the woman, or burden her with unwanted responsibilities.

Rep. Nita Lowey stated that the bill "is not about shielding pregnant women." Rather, she said "it is, and has always been about **undermining freedom of choice**," she said. However, Lowey should consider that the freedom of the mother ends when the freedom of others is infringed upon. Freedom cannot be absolute, with no bounds drawn. Certainly, the living creation that now exists in the mother's womb also has rights. Just as terrorists infringe upon the rights of citizens who are innocently travelling in a plane, so are those mothers who abort their innocent babies simply because they feel the life of another human will be a burden on them:

﴿ وَلَا تَقْتُلُوٓا۟ أَوْلَـٰدَكُمْ خَشْيَةَ إِمْلَـٰقٍ ۖ نَّحْنُ نَرْزُقُهُمْ وَإِيَّاكُمْ ۚ
إِنَّ قَتْلَهُمْ كَانَ خِطْـًٔا كَبِيرًا ﴿٣١﴾ ﴾

And kill not your children for fear of poverty. We provide for them and for you. Surely, the killing of them is a great sin.
[17:31]

Mankind continues to be in a destructive state of confusion and contradiction as long as they refuse to submit to the Creator, and to accept the fact that He knows what is best for His creation. Instead, they prefer to believe that they have the right to choose what is right and wrong in everything, and then proceed to submit to the opinion of one side or the other. Nobody can claim to be free from submitting to something, even if it be the opinions of others, or their ever-changing whims.

﴿ أَرَءَيْتَ مَنِ ٱتَّخَذَ إِلَـٰهَهُۥ هَوَىٰهُ أَفَأَنتَ تَكُونُ عَلَيْهِ وَكِيلًا ﴿٤٣﴾ ﴾

Have you (O Muhammad) **seen him who has taken as his god his own desire? Would you then be a watcher over him?**
[25:43]

According to contemporary humanist values, it is often deemed acceptable to take the life of an unborn child, especially if the baby came about through fornication. However, people start to become concerned with the rights of an unborn child when an independent third party kills the baby while it is still in its mother's womb, as can be witnessed in the Laci and Conner Peterson case. One action is seen as being unjust, whereas the same result is not seen as an injustice in the case of those who have taken the life of a child after having their moment of fun.

The controversy behind the issue of abortion shows that a government, driven by human logic and legislation, has affirmed that unborn children have rights, yet politically correct supporters of the act denied that the bill "was about abortion, pointing to language in the bill that specifically protects those carrying out legal abortions from prosecution."[56] The contradictions abound.

Creating Ethical Limbo

Liberalist ideologies hold that mankind can be left to figure out what is best for itself. However, disturbing contradictions start to appear when these ideologies are implemented. For example, moral values come into mode for a certain amount of time, and then years later, these same moral values which were held to be sacred and correct before, are suddenly overturned and deemed flawed. This necessitates that the particular value system that was originally created by this group was faulty, and that they were living by and believing in something that was incorrect to begin with.

Conversely, these same people will say that something is wrong and immoral one year, and then a decade later, they will deem it to be something that everyone *must* accept as being good and progressive. New legislation is drawn up, and democratically elected politicians rush to bend to the latest social trend, as if they believe wholeheartedly in it; all of this based solely upon the latest opinion polls.

A prime example of this would be the recent changes many societies have taken to accept gay rights. A few decades ago, homosexuality was considered a disorder, whereas now, anyone who holds this view is considered to be suffering from a disorder called homophobia. This new classification puts such an individual in the same category as racists.

At the same time, many of these people who have recently changed their opinions are still hesitant to allow homosexuals the right to legally marry. Is this not from the infringement of peoples' freedom?

Sarah Fulton of *The Queen's United Journal* made an insightful observation, when she noted that almost three in four Americans polled on their opinions pertaining to homosexual rights "supported equal opportunity for employment, as well as protection from prejudice." However, according to Fulton, the same number opposed same-sex marriage.

---

[56] Jim Abrams, House Passes Unborn Victims Legislation, *The Associated Press*, February 26, 2004.

"While the institution of marriage is increasingly becoming questioned throughout North America's heterosexual community," states Fulton, "there is a lingering sentiment for an ideal notion of marriage which precludes homosexual marriage. **But, what is it exactly about same-sex marriage that makes so many people oppose it, though they support homosexual rights?**"[57]

Fulton has grasped the quandary of condoning somebody's way of life, yet at the same time, obstructing him or her from actually applying it. She has also accurately described the exodus of almost all things from the religious to the secular sphere - even sacred matters such as marriage.

The Migration of Ethics From Law

The secularisation of these matters can be attributed to a false distinction that has now been made between moral and legal matters, as if they are two separate entities. For example, *The Catholic World News* reported that Colombia's Constitutional Court, the nation's highest legal entity, "may legalize incest as it considers a request to eliminate the criminal penalty for sexual intercourse between brothers and sisters or parents and children."[58]

Referring to the distinction of making moral and legal matters two separate entities, Alberto Franco, a lawyer pushing for this new legislation, said that incest "**is a moral problem and not a legal one, because it is related to freedom and personal autonomy.**"[59] Franco epitomizes people's obsession with pursuing freedom and personal autonomy, and demonstrates how this drive to endorse unrestrained freedom pushes mankind towards an abyss that knows no boundaries.

Determining Mankind's True Criterion in Resolving Problems

Shaykh Muhammad ibn Saalih al-'Uthaymeen, the great Muslim scholar who died in 2000 (1421H), spoke about how in this time, some people "turn away from Islaam, believing it to be a retrogressive religion that holds people back, acting as a barrier between them and progress."

---

[57] Sarah Fulton, A Question Of Equal Rights, *The Queen's United Journal.*

[58] Colombian Court To Discuss Legalization Of Incest, *Catholic World News*, July 31, 1998.

[59] Ibid.

Said Ibn Uthaymeen: "Islaam does not restrict freedom, but it is a means of regulating and channelling it in the correct way, such that the freedom of one person does not clash with the freedom of another. This is what occurs when freedom is granted without boundaries, because any person who desires absolute freedom without any boundaries will inevitably fulfil this at the expense of other people's freedom. As a result of this, discord occurs when people's freedoms clash, chaos spreads and corruption sets in. It is for this reason that Allaah named the injunctions of the religion "limits" (*hudood*)...

...Therefore, there is a difference between the restriction of freedoms that this group of people assume, and the channelling and regulating of these freedoms that the Most Wise, the Most Acquainted, legislates for His servants.

Consequently, there is no reason to raise such an issue, as systematisation is a reality in all domains, and man is by nature submissive to this systematic reality. He is submissive to the sway of hunger and thirst, and to the organization of his food and drink. Thus, he is forced to organize his food and drink as far as quantity, quality and type is concerned, so that he may safeguard his health and welfare.

In the same way, he is submissive to the system that his society lays out for him, holding on to the customs of his country in his dwellings, garb and modes of transport... If he does not subject himself to this system, he will be considered as being abnormal, and he will be treated in the way abnormal people are treated.

Consequently, life is by nature a form of submission to specified limits, so that everything may progress according to its intended purpose. Since this submission to a social system is something necessary in order to maintain the integrity of the community and prevent chaos, similarly, submission to the system of Islaamic legislation [in matters of worship and dealings] is a necessary matter for the uprightness of the Islaamic nation. So how is it that some people become dissatisfied with it and deem it to be something which restricts their freedom? Verily, this is a great untruth and a false, evil presumption.

Furthermore, Islaam does not suppress people's capabilities. On the contrary, it is a comprehensive way of life that encourages physical, rational and intellectual advancement ...

...Islaam calls people to reasoning and reflection, so that mankind may contemplate, and their minds and thoughts may develop... However, it does not confine itself to calling towards contemplation and deep thought. Rather, it also denounces those who do not observe, contemplate and use their sense of reason.

Allaah the Most High says:

﴿ أَوَلَمْ يَنظُرُوا۟ فِى مَلَكُوتِ ٱلسَّمَـٰوَٰتِ وَٱلْأَرْضِ وَمَا خَلَقَ ٱللَّهُ مِن شَىْءٍ ﴾

"Do they not look in the dominion of the heavens and the earth and everything that Allaah has created?"
[7:185]

And Allaah the Most High says:

﴿ أَوَلَمْ يَتَفَكَّرُوا۟ فِىٓ أَنفُسِهِم ۗ مَّا خَلَقَ ٱللَّهُ ٱلسَّمَـٰوَٰتِ
وَٱلْأَرْضَ وَمَا بَيْنَهُمَآ إِلَّا بِٱلْحَقِّ وَأَجَلٍ مُّسَمًّى ﴾

Do they not reflect upon the creation of their own selves? Allaah did not create the heavens and the earth, and all that is between them, except in truth, and for an appointed term.
[30:8]

The order to observe and ponder is but an unfastening of the mind's ability to think and reason; so how can some people say that it restricts people's capabilities?

﴿ كَبُرَتْ كَلِمَةً تَخْرُجُ مِنْ أَفْوَٰهِهِمْ ۚ إِن يَقُولُونَ إِلَّا كَذِبًا ﴾

Mighty is the word that issues forth from their mouths. They utter nothing but a lie.
[18:5]

For Islaam has indeed rendered lawful for its adherents all things which do not harm the individual's body, religion or intellect..."[60]

[60] Shaykh Muhammad ibn Saalih al-'Uthaymeen, *Min Mushkilaat ash-Shabaab*, pp. 21-25, *Daarul-Manaar*.

Safeguarding Legitimate Rights and Freedoms

An objective examination of the previously mentioned issues can help people conclude that the Creator has safeguarded the rights and freedoms of both individuals and societies. Nobody's personal freedom is allowed to infringe on the freedom of other individuals, or more importantly, the welfare of mankind. Furthermore, nobody has the true insight to truthfully determine what is beneficial or corrupting for individuals and societies as a whole, except the Creator who originated these individuals and societies. For that reason, nobody except Allaah can accurately grant rights and freedoms, or set limits for these rights and freedoms - no matter how intelligent or advanced these people and their societies are.

Indeed, the moral freedoms the West has delved into have caused many Westerners to live a life of fear and insecurity. Due to the entertainment industry's glorification of crime and violence, many people feel the consequences of this liberal way of life in their daily existence. This is only one of the effects that extremist views in advocating freedom have upon society as a whole.

These undefined outlooks towards freedom have a deep impact on individual lives. In liberal societies, people attempt to find true satisfaction by engaging in a wide variety of endeavours. However, many honest people living this reality recognize that there is still something crucial missing in their lives, even though many of their activities might actually be beneficial in nature. What these people are feeling is an instinctive yearning the Creator has placed within them to know that they were created to worship and serve the Creator, even when carrying out their day-to-day activities.

People who turn away from their natural disposition to realize this matter often suffer from bouts of worry and depression, as is witnessed in the high suicide rates found in liberal countries. Indeed, liberal lifestyles help create temporary forms of satisfaction, but are instrumental in keeping people away from what their Creator has ordained for them. Although mankind is capable of discovering temporary forms of contentment in life, our limited ability to perceive absolute truth by ourselves keeps us from knowing how to achieve true and lasting satisfaction in this life and the next. Contrary to this limited cognisance is the all-encompassing knowledge of the One who knows all that has passed, all that will pass, and how all the things that never passed would have been, had they passed:

﴿ يَعْلَمُ مَا بَيْنَ أَيْدِيهِمْ وَمَا خَلْفَهُمْ ۖ وَلَا يُحِيطُونَ بِشَيْءٍ مِّنْ عِلْمِهِۦٓ إِلَّا بِمَا شَآءَ ﴾

He knows what happens to them in this world, and what will happen to them in the Hereafter. And they will never compass anything of His Knowledge, except that which He wills.
[2:255]

In this era, many people follow humanist conjecture and seek out various forms of worship in a mistaken bid to satisfy their natural yearnings to worship and serve the Creator. This failed effort causes many people to hold on to the religion they found their forefathers following in a nominal way, accepting and rejecting from it whatever they want. Many present-day Jews and Christians react to their religions in this manner, due primarily to their awareness that the beliefs they inherited contain human additions and deletions which came about through time and historical experience.

Some people reject formal religions entirely, not realizing that their liberalist beliefs also constitute a set of religious beliefs that they apply in their lives. Others turn to experimentation with exotic religions and philosophies such as Buddhism and Yoga, or become completely immersed in fanatical cults of one sort or another.

Those who prefer to conjecture in religious matters or turn away from God completely actually cover their natural disposition in this regard and deprive themselves of the opportunity to experience ultimate satisfaction. Just as our bodies have certain natural needs such as the need to eat and drink, our Creator has also endowed us with an innate drive to worship and serve Him. As such, true, lasting contentment can only come about through remembrance of the Creator in the manner he has prescribed, and sincerity of purpose to Him:

﴿ ٱلَّذِينَ ءَامَنُواْ وَتَطْمَئِنُّ قُلُوبُهُم بِذِكْرِ ٱللَّهِ ۗ أَلَا بِذِكْرِ ٱللَّهِ تَطْمَئِنُّ ٱلْقُلُوبُ ﴿٢٨﴾ ﴾

Those who believed, and whose hearts find rest in the remembrance of Allaah: Verily, in the remembrance of Allaah do hearts find rest.
[13:28]

People who turn away from the revealed way of the Creator eventually end up living a life of doubt, unease and irresolution, even if their easy going ways give the impression that they are content.

﴿ وَمَنْ أَعْرَضَ عَن ذِكْرِى فَإِنَّ لَهُۥ مَعِيشَةً ضَنكًا وَنَحْشُرُهُۥ يَوْمَ ٱلْقِيَـٰمَةِ أَعْمَىٰ ﴿١٢٤﴾ قَالَ رَبِّ لِمَ حَشَرْتَنِىٓ أَعْمَىٰ وَقَدْ كُنتُ بَصِيرًا ﴿١٢٥﴾ قَالَ كَذَٰلِكَ أَتَتْكَ ءَايَـٰتُنَا فَنَسِيتَهَا ۖ وَكَذَٰلِكَ ٱلْيَوْمَ تُنسَىٰ ﴿١٢٦﴾ ﴾

But whosoever turns away from My Reminder, verily, for him is a life of hardship, and We shall raise him up blind on the Day of Resurrection.

He will say: "O my Lord! Why have you raised me up blind, while I had sight (before)?"

(Allaah) will say: "Thus did Our Signs come to you, but you disregarded them; and so will you, this Day, be disregarded."
[20:124-126]

Ibn Katheer (d.1372, 774H), the famous commentator of the *Qur'aan*, stated that the verse **"Whosoever turns away from My Reminder"** means: "Contradicts My command and what I sent down to My prophet by turning away from this guidance and purposely neglecting it, adopting the guidance of others: **"For him is a life of hardship,"** meaning, whoever does this will experience a troubled life in this world, as he will never feel true peace of mind or comfort. On the contrary, he will experience discontent and anxiety due to his straying from the right path, even if he appears to lead a life of comfort and ease by eating, drinking, dressing and residing in the way he desires. As long as his heart has not arrived at certainty of belief and true guidance, he will be living a life of worry, doubt and confusion, wavering in a state of uncertainty."

Ibn 'Abbaas, the Prophet Muhammad's (ﷺ) companion, said the following regarding this verse: "A people who were living a life of affluence and arrogance strayed from the right path by turning away from the truth. They were living a life of hardship due to their notion that Allaah (created them, but) is somehow not involved in providing them their sustenance. (This belief of self-sufficiency) stemmed from their negative opinion and denial towards Him. For if a person rejects Allaah, holds false suspicions and mistrusts Him, his life becomes difficult and restricted, and that is the hardship (which Allaah has referred to)."[61]

[61] *Tafseer Ibn Katheer, Daarul-Andalus*, vol.4, p.544.

Indeed, Islaam prevents personal and societal disorders before they have the chance to occur, thus protecting and channelling mankind's legitimate rights and freedoms in a more effective manner.

It can be concluded that there is no such thing as absolute freedom, as all freedom has bounds. Who then, is given the right to set these boundaries, and why? When people differ in matters which affect mankind, who is it that decides what is right and wrong? One person believes something to be from people's freedom, while others disagree. If not Allaah, the Most Acquainted and All-Knowing Planner of all, then **who else should mankind refer to** in deciding these crucial matters, and **what will their criterion be in doing so**? Can mankind decide everything for themselves?

﴿ قُلْ ءَأَنتُمْ أَعْلَمُ أَمِ ٱللَّهُ ﴾

Say (to them), "Do you know better or does Allaah?"
[2:140]

People who objectively consider all the variables involved in these matters will be led to conclude that mankind cannot lay claim to absolute freedom. Furthermore, they will also conclude that manmade resolutions which oppose authentic revelation are contradictory, continually changing and inherently faulty. As such, they are not universally applicable, as their adherents claim. Manmade solutions might create temporary ease in some matters and appear to some to be more appealing than divine legislation, however, the truth lies with those who refer their affairs back to their Creator, and render His revelation their criterion in making any decisions which affect mankind's well being.

﴿ وَمَا يَتَّبِعُ أَكْثَرُهُمْ إِلَّا ظَنًّا ۚ إِنَّ ٱلظَّنَّ لَا يُغْنِى مِنَ
ٱلْحَقِّ شَيْـًٔا ۚ إِنَّ ٱللَّهَ عَلِيمٌۢ بِمَا يَفْعَلُونَ ﴿٣٦﴾ ﴾

And most of them follow nothing but conjecture.
Certainly, conjecture can be of no avail against the truth.
Surely, Allaah is All-Aware of what they do.
[10:36]

Is Democracy the Answer to Mankind's Woes?

Liberalism and Democracy Through Occupation and Coercion

In an article entitled "Cheney: Nations Must Join in Terror Fight," *The Associated Press'* Deb Riechmann quoted Dick Cheney, the United States' Vice President, as saying: "Ideologies of violence must be confronted at the source by nurturing democracy throughout the Middle East and beyond."[62]

According to a speech given by President George Bush that he gave to the National Endowment for Democracy (NED),[63] Bush said that democracy in Muslim nations "must be a focus of American policy for decades to come."

---

[62] Deb Riechmann, Cheney: Nations Must Join in Terror Fight, *The Associated Press*, January 24, 2004.

[63] Barbara Conry, a foreign policy analyst at the Cato Institute in Washington, D.C., had the following to say about the National Endowment for Democracy: "NED, which also has a history of corruption and financial mismanagement, is superfluous at best and often destructive. Through the endowment," argues Conry, "the American taxpayer has paid for special-interest groups to harass the duly elected governments of friendly countries, interfere in foreign elections, and foster the corruption of democratic movements." (Barbara Conry, Loose Cannon: The National Endowment for Democracy, Cato Foreign Policy Briefing No. 27, November 8, 1993.)

After mentioning that NED had interfered in the election process of France, Portugal and Spain, William Blum explained how NED "successfully manipulated elections in Nicaragua in 1990 and Mongolia in 1996 and helped to overthrow democratically elected governments in Bulgaria in 1990 and Albania in 1991 and 1992."

Likewise, NED has been instrumental in trying to force out democratically elected governments in Haiti and Venezuela. Both President Jean-Bertrand Aristide and President Hugo Chavez had their leadership challenged through the support of NED funding of opposition groups. These violent coups against democratically elected governments were publicized as being triumphs for the cause of democracy. In reality, they were acts of destabilization that Blum termed as being "in sync with the basic needs and objectives of the New World Order's economic globalization."

In short, the call to democracy is often nothing but a front for the promotion and preservation of the interests of the financial elite. In spite of this, the common masses believe that their interests are best represented and preserved by making democracy an unquestionable ideology.

One by one, nations are being lined up for pre-emptive strikes and wars of "liberation." Democracy will be part of what Bush calls a "forward strategy of freedom in the Middle East." Said Bush: "The establishment of a free Iraq in the heart of the Middle East will be a watershed event in the global democratic revolution."[64]

In actuality, a complete book could be written about the true motives behind the drive for war and democracy in the Middle East. Rather than look into the true objectives behind these efforts, an examination of the legitimacy of the fundamentals of democracy will prove to be more beneficial, as democracy seems to have been raised to an almost sacred status.

The Realities of Democracy

Although democracy might appear to some as being a terrific ideology that everyone should follow, its true reality speaks differently. Democracy holds that the right of judgment lies with the people, and not the Creator. As previously discussed, this kind of belief entails that mankind is wiser and more knowledgeable than the Creator, something that is not logically acceptable.

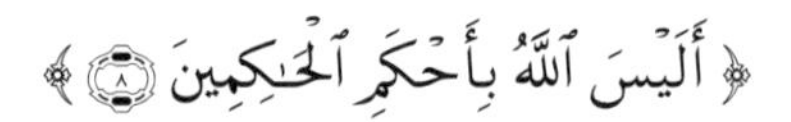

Is not Allaah the wisest of Judges?
[95:8]

Another deficiency that can be found within democracy is that it enables everybody to have an avenue to express his or her "opinion." Although this might appear to some to be a good thing, in reality, this ideology allows everyone - including unintelligent, uninformed and insincere people - the right to control mankind's future. Democracy holds the view that millions of people are wiser than one, which caused one Western thinker to state that Democracy is "a pathetic belief in the collective wisdom of individual ignorance."

On November 2, 2004, *The Herald*'s Ian Bell wrote an article exposing the flaws of the Democratic process in America. Titling his article "Next

[64] President Bush Discusses Freedom in Iraq and Middle East, *The White House: Office of the Press Secretary*, November 6, 2003.

US leader to be decided by 'voters ignorant beyond belief,'" Bell based his editorial upon the confessions of Peter Oborne, a right-wing journalist who surprisingly criticized the American democratic process on British television.[65] According to Oborne's account, Bell mentions that the 2004 presidential campaign "would be decided by a small, decisive, yet 'largely ignorant' group of manipulated voters."

According to Bell, "none of those interviewed could find Iraq or Afghanistan on the map."

"Asked to identify Britain," stated Bell, "one man pointed to West Africa." Another, with his finger on North Korea, said: "Afghanistan is over here, where Russia used to be."

Westerners often resent Islaam's classification of people on the basis of belief, yet they themselves classify those who adhere to their beliefs as being "civilized," and those who have not yet adopted these values as being "uncivilized." If the aforementioned accounts are examples of democracy in what has been described by Westerners as the civilized world, what could be said about the implementation of democracy in what Westerners consider to be the uncivilized world, where most people have little or no education?

Although Bell does not share the same staunch political conservatism as Oborne, both of them have come to agree about America's intent to spread democracy around the world: "Judging on how it works at home," Bell quoted Oborne as saying, "we should all be very afraid."[66]

﴿ وَإِن تُطِعْ أَكْثَرَ مَن فِي ٱلْأَرْضِ يُضِلُّوكَ عَن سَبِيلِ ٱللَّهِ ۚ
إِن يَتَّبِعُونَ إِلَّا ٱلظَّنَّ وَإِنْ هُمْ إِلَّا يَخْرُصُونَ ﴿١١٦﴾ ﴾

And if you were to obey most of those on earth, they would mislead you far away from Allaah's Way. They follow nothing but conjecture, and they do nothing but guess.
[6:116]

[65] Peter Oborne, The Dirty Race for the White House, *Channel 4*, November 1, 2004, 8:00 P.M.

[66] Ian Bell, *The Herald*, Next US leader to be decided by 'voters ignorant beyond belief,' November 2, 2004.

An All-Knowing and All-Wise Creator has informed us that if we were to follow the ever-changing opinions of the majority, they would certainly mislead us. People who are not grounded in the knowledge of what their Creator wills them to do - no matter how knowledgeable they may be in certain other worldly affairs - fall under the category of those who mislead people **"far away from Allaah's Path."**

People who contradict their Creator's guidance "**follow nothing but conjecture, and they do nothing but guess.**" Their opinions are based on fleeting preferences that never remain constant. As such, their conjecture leads them to speak untruthfully, either out of ignorance, or due to the following of their desires.

Furthermore, many of those who favour democracy as an ideology are still ready to concede that the old saying, "all politicians are liars," is true. In his article on the American presidential campaign of 2004, Ian Bell spoke about the "dirty race for the White House," stating that John Kerry tried to appease the "gun nuts of West Virginia after voting for gun control 55 times." Speaking about how the campaign was "based on fear, lies and black propaganda," Bell states that both sides "lie about their lies."[67]

Making false promises and lying is encouraged in the democratic political system in order to achieve authority. How then could it ever be considered a truthful, correct or morally superior ideology, never mind one that everyone in the world must apply - or else face war?

A Lurking Threat to Mankind

Although Western democracy does allow the electorate the ability to choose whom their leaders will be, they are in actuality given very little choice in what ideological course their countries will take. For example, the difference between the British Conservative and Labour parties is minimal, just as the difference between the American Democrats and Republicans is also nominal.

Although parties of differing ideological inclinations are allowed to participate in the democratic process, they are often only tolerated so long as they are considered non-threatening, marginal forces. If they begin to develop a majority of support - such as what happened to the Algerian party

[67] Ibid.

FIS (the political-activist movement that sought democratic means of establishing a supposed Islaamic government) - those who were preaching freedom and democracy will suddenly disregard the belief of majority rule in order to preserve the status quo, which they term freedom of choice. Hence, the notion of democratic rule and freedom of choice is much more controlled than people might assume.

Scarier than this is the realization that democracy can create a state that would be just as oppressive as any fascist state. All the different forms of personal freedom that people believe in are derived from the opinion of the majority. If the opinion of the majority is swayed to deem that a certain minority of people should be detained en-masse,[68] or even that they be eliminated, this could certainly become a reality. This is what occurred when fascist Nazi leaders and their media convinced common Germans in World War II that the Jews and Gypsies should be eradicated. Since democracy maintains that there is **no particular set truth or absolute criterion that should be referred to besides the opinion of the majority**, it is completely conceivable that the likes of this could occur.

In an interview with Amy Goodman of *Democracy Now*, *The New Yorker*'s Seymour Hersh referred to the tie that exists between the media and contemporary democratic rule in America. Stating that America has been "taken over basically by a cult," Hersh commented that eight or nine neo-conservatives "have somehow grabbed the government."

"Just how and why and how [sic] they did it so efficiently, will have to wait for much later historians and better documentation than we have now," stated Hersh. "They managed to overcome the bureaucracy and the Congress, and [sic] the press, with the greatest of ease. It does say something about how fragile our Democracy is," added Hersh.

---

[68] This has already occurred in a democratically represented nation. During the Second World War, Japanese citizens were rounded up en-masse in American concentration camps.

More recently, *The Associated Press* reported that in a poll conducted by Cornell University, "nearly half of all Americans believe the U.S. government should restrict the civil liberties of Muslim-Americans." (*The Associated Press*, Poll shows U.S. views on Muslim Americans, December 17, 2004.)

With 44 percent of Americans favouring these restrictions of civil liberties, the democratic majority needed to implement these ideas is not far removed.

Referring to the reality of democracy and how it can become a hidden form of autocracy, Hersh stated: "You do have to wonder what a Democracy is when it comes down to a few men in the Pentagon and a few men in the White House having their way."

The manufacturing of consent within a democratic system cannot occur without the aid of the media. Since the media essentially controls the sway of public opinion, whoever is able to control or manipulate the media will in actuality be the leader of democratic society.

On March 19, 2004, *The Associated Press*' Mielikki Org reported that a conference on media coverage concluded that competitive pressures and fear of appearing unpatriotic discouraged journalists from doing more critical reporting during the run-up to the invasion of Iraq.

"The press did not do their job," said Michael Massing, author of an article in *The New York Review of Books* that was critical of *The New York Times* and *The Washington Post* in this regard.

Robert Sheer, a syndicated columnist for *The Los Angeles Times*, feels that journalists fear they will be seen as unpatriotic if they challenge White House statements: "There is no doubt that there is an **atmosphere of fear in the media** of being out of sync with the punitive government," he said.[69]

When a democratic nation applies oppressive measures to anyone at home or abroad, these measures will most often only be removed once it is deemed that there are too many financial or political drawbacks (such as casualties) involved in continuing this oppression. This situation is able to arise because **democracy does not recognize any absolute values besides the ever-changing opinions of the masses**. This type of realization caused one Western thinker to state that tyranny and despotism "can be exercised by many, more rigorously, and more severely, than by one."

Democracy Encourages Seeking Fame and Authority

During the month of February 2004, a great debate was created when Gavin Newsom, the mayor of San Francisco, ordered city officials to allow gay marriages. As a result, thousands of homosexual couples rushed to get

[69] Mielikki Org, Fears Impacted U.S. Reporting on Iraq, *The Associated Press,* March 19, 2004.

married. Newsom, who was going against state law, defended his position by saying: "What matters is doing the right thing and being true to yourself and standing up on principle."

However, according to Lisa Leff of *The Associated Press*, the thing "that really matters to Mayor Gavin Newsom is what they're saying in the neighborhoods of San Francisco - that his decision to buck California law and grant marriage licenses to gay and lesbian couples makes him a hero."[70]

Although Newsom feels that he has taken this position by "doing the right thing," "being true" to himself and "standing up on principle," what really matters to him is what his constituency is saying, as homosexuality is known to be more widespread in San Francisco than in any other major city of the United States. Following the opinions of his electorate and defending them will ensure that he is seen as being a hero, and consequently, that he will be assured status, reputation and leadership in the land.

Demonstrating the confusion and contradiction which abounds when mankind is left to decide what is to be considered morally acceptable, *The Associated Press* quoted James Warren, a San Francisco judge, as saying that San Francisco "appears to be violating the law by issuing marriage licenses to gay and lesbian couples."

Robert Tyler, a lawyer for a group called the Alliance Defense Fund, requested the Superior Court judge issue an order to stop the city from issuing homosexuals marriage licenses. Referring directly to this social disorder, he said, **"This is municipal anarchy."**

Governor Arnold Schwarzenegger, the democratically elected leader of California and star of such films as The Terminator, "urged city officials to stop the same-sex weddings." However, before doing that, he did protect his political standing by saying: "I support all of California's existing laws that provide domestic partnership benefits and protections." After completing this politically correct statement, he then said, "However, Californians spoke on the issue of same-sex marriage when they overwhelmingly approved California's law that defines marriage as being between a man and a woman."

---

[70] Lisa Leff, S.F. Mayor Happy With Marriage Decision, *The Associated Press*, February 21, 2004.

Hence, it can be understood from Schwarzenegger's comments that he supports homosexual rights, yet opposes same-sex marriage, solely on the basis that "Californians spoke on the issue."[71] Schwarzenegger's **reference point** in arriving at this important conclusion was **the opinion of the majority.** As such, if the majority were to change back and forth with different decisions, so would the opinion of Governor Schwarzenegger.

Seeking Fame and Authority: A Corrupting Force

The final Prophet (ﷺ) forbade seeking authority, as it is something that corrupts the individual and those he rules. The Prophet (ﷺ) said: "*You people will be keen to acquire the authority of leadership, but it will be a thing of regret for you on the Day of Resurrection.*"[72]

In another *hadeeth*, he (ﷺ) said: "O *'Abdur-Rahmaan! Do not ask for leadership, for if you are given authority on your demand, then you will be held responsible for it, but if you are given it without asking (for it), then you will be helped (by Allaah) in it.*"[73]

Not only did he forbid from asking for authority and leadership, he even forbade people from desiring it in their inner selves - so much so is the corrupting element of these desires. Abu Moosaa al-Ash'aree (رضي الله عنه), the Companion of the Prophet (ﷺ), narrated the following account: "Two men from my tribe and I entered upon the Prophet. One of the two men said (to him), "O Messenger of Allaah! Appoint me as a governor," and so did the second. The Prophet said, "*We do not assign the authority of ruling to those who ask for it, nor to those who are keen to have it.*"[74]

In his book, "The Methodology of the Prophets in calling to Allaah; That is the Way of Wisdom and Intelligence," Shaykh Rabee' ibn Haadee al-Madkhalee made the following comment about how people should be selected for positions within an Islaamic government: "It is essential that we follow the methodology of Allaah's Messenger (ﷺ) in choosing the governors and the judges. These positions are not to be given to those who

---

[71] David Kravets and Lisa Leff, Judge Says Gay Marriages Appear Illegal, *Associated Press*, February 18, 2004.

[72] Related by al-Bukhaaree, (no. 7148), Eng. Trans.

[73] Ibid, (no. 7146)

[74] Ibid, (no. 7149)

ask for them, or desire them, **or put themselves forward for them in elections**, for example, **as this is (to be considered) from the desiring of these positions.**"

"Rather," he continued, "the ones to be chosen are those who are suitable in knowledge, abstention, and piety." Shaykh Rabee' advised against the ways of the political-activist groups and movements of today, saying, "We should not bring up the youth to have love for position, authority, ascendancy and leadership. If we bring them up upon love of these things, then we will have acted contrary to the guidance of Allaah's Messenger (ﷺ), and will have led the youth to that which will bring about their destruction."[75]

Democracy necessitates people leaving off the guidance of the Creator for the contradictory ways of His created beings. Furthermore, democracy is based upon the craving of status, position and authority, often involving lying and deceit. Most of mankind's problems are based upon people competing with each other for leadership and status. Although democracy appears to some to be advantageous, a closer examination of its fundamental principles proves that it corrupts individuals and societies as a whole.

Contrary to this is the Islaamic system of *shooraa*, or consultation, in which the Islaamic leader consults specialists in their respective fields of religious or worldly knowledge. Our All-Wise Creator has praised those **"who (conduct) their affairs by mutual consultation,"**[76] and He ordered His Messenger (ﷺ) to consult with his Companions, saying:

﴿ وَشَاوِرْهُمْ فِي ٱلْأَمْرِ ۖ فَإِذَا عَزَمْتَ فَتَوَكَّلْ عَلَى ٱللَّهِ ۚ إِنَّ ٱللَّهَ يُحِبُّ ٱلْمُتَوَكِّلِينَ ﴿١٥٩﴾ ﴾

And consult them (O Muhammad) in the matter:
Then when you have taken a decision, put your trust in Allaah.
Certainly, Allaah loves those who put their trust (in Him).
[3:159]

As a result of this consultative process that returns mankind's affairs to the firmly established fundamentals mentioned at the beginning of this

[75] Shaykh Rabee' ibn Haadee al-Madkhalee, *Manhajul-Anbiyaa' fid-Da'wah il-Allaah Feehil-Hikmah wal-'Aql, Maktabatul-Furqaan*, pp.125, 126.

[76] The *Qur'aan* 42:38

book,[77] they avoid following conjecture. Therefore, how can it be considered that an ideology which encourages flattery, rehearsed poses, empty slogans, stage-managed political rallies packed with party loyalists, smear campaigns, lying and ever-changing opinions, be better than the Way of the Lord of the worlds?

﴿ فَمَاذَا بَعْدَ ٱلْحَقِّ إِلَّا ٱلضَّلَٰلُ ۖ فَأَنَّىٰ تُصْرَفُونَ ﴾

So after the truth, what else can there be, save error?
How then are you turned away?
[10:32]

[77] The first three chapters have dealt with the subjects of the existence of a Creator, why He alone deserves to be worshipped and served in our lives, and how He has sent down revelation which shows us how this worship and servitude should be carried out.

Is Secularism a Sound Ideology?

Does Secularism Exist in the Bible?

Because of the historical difficulties Christians have experienced in their dealings with the Church, many Christians hold a deep sense of animosity towards the interference of religion in their lives. However, it is important to understand that Westerners have arrived at their present state due to their encounters with their own religious authorities. As such, deductions made from Western historical experiences cannot always be applied on a universal basis, especially when considering that Muslims' material progress went hand in hand with their adherence to religion. Therefore, it should not be thought that Christian society came to these contemporary secularist conclusions through a truly objective process.

In a *New York Times'* article taken from his book *The Crisis of Islam*, Bernard Lewis attempted to show how Jesus (عليه السلام), unlike Muhammad (ﷺ), was able to separate religion and state. Quoting from The New Testament, Lewis stated that Jesus "bade his followers 'render unto Caesar the things which are Caesar's; and unto God the things which are God's.'"[78]

In order to give Christians the idea that Jesus (عليه السلام) was actually an early supporter of secularism, Lewis has turned to religious scripture, hoping that he can find something within the message of the prophets that might validate modern secularist belief. However, this effort can be disproved from several perspectives.

Firstly, Lewis is quoting from the Gospel of Matthew. A closer look at the authenticity of the New Testament shows that the authors of the four Gospels are unknown and are not believed to have met Jesus (عليه السلام). Based upon historical and theological accounts, the *Encyclopaedia Britannica* states the following regarding the Gospel According to Matthew: "... the

[78] Bernard Lewis, The Crisis of Islam, *The New York Times*, April 6, 2003.

writer of Matthew is probably anonymous."[79] Regarding the Gospel According to Mark, it states: "Though the author of Mark is probably unknown..."[80] Likewise is the case of the author of the Gospel According to Luke: "In short, the author of this gospel remains unknown."[81] The true identity of the writer of the Gospel According to John is also unknown: "From internal evidence, the Gospel was written by a beloved disciple whose name is unknown."[82]

The Gospel that Jesus (عليه السلام) had been sent with later became lost and was replaced by the Gospel *according to* Matthew, Mark, Luke and John. Complicating things further, many Bible scholars acknowledge that the authors of these gospels are unknown. For this reason, Lewis cannot use this verse as an absolute proof that Jesus (عليه السلام) actually ever said such a thing, as "the writer of Matthew is probably anonymous."[83] Besides which, it seems quite ironic that someone who is trying to prove a point about secularism would need to turn to religious scripture to try to achieve his objective.

Secondly, were we to assume that Jesus (عليه السلام) actually said, "Render unto Caesar the things which are Caesar's; and unto God the things which are God's"[84] - and that it was not a later fabrication - the context of the statement needs to be considered:

> "Then the Pharisees went and took counsel how to entangle him in his talk. And they sent their disciples to him, along with the Hero'dians, saying, "Teacher, we know that you are true, and teach the way of God truthfully, and care for no man; for you do not regard the position of men. Tell us, then, what you think. Is it lawful to pay taxes to Caesar, or not?" But Jesus, aware of their malice, said, "Why put me to the test, you hypocrites? Show me the money for the tax." And they brought him a coin. And Jesus said to them, "Whose like-

---

[79] *The New Encyclopaedia Britannica* (Chicago: Helen Hemingway Benton Publishers, 1980), vol. 2, p.953.

[80] Ibid, vol. 2, p.951.

[81] Ibid, vol. 2, p.954.

[82] Ibid, vol. 2, p.955.

[83] Ibid, vol. 2, p.953.

[84] Matthew 22:21

ness and inscription is this?" They said, "Caesar's." Then he said to them, "Render therefore to Caesar the things that are Caesar's, and to God the things that are God's." When they heard it, they marveled; and they left him and went away." (Matthew 22:15-22)

From this quotation of Matthew, we can observe that Jesus was reported to have been tested by the Pharisees about the matter of paying taxes to the Romans. Perceiving their plot, Jesus (عليه السلام) reportedly answered them by telling them to pay their taxes, when he said, "Render therefore to Caesar the things that are Caesar's, and to God the things that are God's." How this verse - which is dealing with the subject of paying taxes - can be used as a proof to discard the legislation of the Creator is beyond comprehension.

Thirdly, another verse exists in the same book of Matthew that Lewis quoted from which is clearer in meaning than the one he has tried to use as a proof. This other verse obviously contradicts his claim that Jesus was a supporter of secularism, as it clearly states that Jesus did not come to change or secularize the law of the prophets: "Think not that I have come to destroy the law, or the prophets: I am not come to destroy but to fulfill." (Matthew 5:17)

﴿ يَٰٓأَهۡلَ ٱلۡكِتَٰبِ لِمَ تَلۡبِسُونَ ٱلۡحَقَّ بِٱلۡبَٰطِلِ وَتَكۡتُمُونَ ٱلۡحَقَّ وَأَنتُمۡ تَعۡلَمُونَ ﴾

O people of the Scripture: Why do you mix truth with falsehood and conceal the truth while you know?

[3:71]

Marginalizing the Creator's Religion

On November 2, 2001, *The New York Times* allowed Salman Rushdie the opportunity to invite Muslims to marginalize their faith. In his article entitled, "Yes, This is About Islam," Rushdie wrote the following about Muslim writers and intellectuals who have embraced secularist-humanist beliefs: "If Islam is to be reconciled with modernity, these voices must be encouraged until they swell into a roar." Rushdie then speaks about how Muslims should discard the majority of their religion and relegate Islaam to the realm of a marginalized, personal faith: "Many of them speak of another Islam, their personal, private faith."[85]

[85] Salman Rushdie, Yes, This is About Islam, *The New York Times*, November 2, 2001.

It can be understood from Rushdie's article that adhering to Islaam in its entirety can only be done grudgingly. However, would it be reasonable to believe that an All-Wise Creator - who has created in the best of ways - would really ordain a way of life that causes unhappiness, or would fail to put all aspects of worship and human interpersonal dealings in their appropriate place?

﴿ مَا قَدَرُواْ ٱللَّهَ حَقَّ قَدْرِهِۦٓۗ إِنَّ ٱللَّهَ لَقَوِىٌّ عَزِيزٌ ﴿٧٤﴾ ﴾

No just estimate have they made of Allaah.
Verily, Allaah is All-Strong, All-Mighty.
[22:74]

People who turn away from the guidance of the Creator either follow some sort of formal man-made religion or philosophy, or follow a religion which was originally revealed by the Creator, but later became altered. Others have become disillusioned with these formal religions, moving from one type of personal conjecture to another.

Islaam liberates people from these types of beliefs. The Islaamic system of belief links the believer to his Creator through a series of easily observable rites of worship that purify the soul. Since the Creator's knowledge is all-encompassing, it should not come as a surprise that He would legislate a complete religion that includes both matters related to worship as well as matters related to dealings between His creation. Likewise, because the Creator is free of making error, it should not be surprising that He wants His created beings to submit to Him by following His legislated way in all matters:

﴿ يَـٰٓأَيُّهَا ٱلَّذِينَ ءَامَنُواْ ٱدْخُلُواْ فِى ٱلسِّلْمِ كَآفَّةً ﴾

O you who believe! Enter into Islaam completely.
[2:208]

Because our Creator is Appreciative and capable of rewarding His servants in this life and the hereafter, anyone who yields to all aspects of His revelation can expect to feel sweetness and joy in their submission to Him. Instead of living an existence of emptiness, discontent and anxiety, a sincere follower of the Creator's legislated way feels a strong sense of peace, tranquility and clarity, free of worry and confusion.[86]

---

[86] Shaykh Muhammad ibn Saalih al-'Uthaymeen, *Sharh Usool al-Eemaan*, p. 61, *Daarul-Watn lin-Nashr.*

﴿ يَٰٓأَيُّهَا ٱلنَّاسُ قَدۡ جَآءَتۡكُم مَّوۡعِظَةٞ مِّن رَّبِّكُمۡ وَشِفَآءٞ
لِّمَا فِي ٱلصُّدُورِ وَهُدٗى وَرَحۡمَةٞ لِّلۡمُؤۡمِنِينَ ٥٧ ﴾

O mankind! There has come to you an admonition from your Lord, and a healing for that which is in the breasts; a guidance and a mercy for the believers.
[10:57]

What Rushdie is inviting Muslims to believe in is that they should follow the desires of those who believe that God exists, but neglectfully failed to establish a way for them to live by. However, does it make logical sense to believe that the Creator brought about this whole magnificent universe from nothing, sustains each necessary atom and molecule within the whole of creation, controls their movements and administrates their affairs with complete wisdom, and at the same time, does not know what mankind is doing or what is best for them?

﴿ أَلَا يَعۡلَمُ مَنۡ خَلَقَ وَهُوَ ٱللَّطِيفُ ٱلۡخَبِيرُ ﴾

"Should He not know, He that created? And He is the One who is Most Kind and Courteous to His Servants, All-Aware."
[67:14]

The One who is most aware of what He created and why, has informed his creation about the following condition of faith for those who claim to believe in Him and the Last Day:

﴿ فَإِن تَنَٰزَعۡتُمۡ فِي شَيۡءٖ فَرُدُّوهُ إِلَى ٱللَّهِ وَٱلرَّسُولِ إِن كُنتُمۡ تُؤۡمِنُونَ
بِٱللَّهِ وَٱلۡيَوۡمِ ٱلۡأٓخِرِۚ ذَٰلِكَ خَيۡرٞ وَأَحۡسَنُ تَأۡوِيلًا ٥٩ ﴾

"And if you differ in anything amongst yourselves, refer the matter back to Allaah and His Messenger, if indeed you believe in Allaah and the Last Day. That is better (for you in this world and the Hereafter), **and better in its final determination."**
[4:59]

The Creator's statement **"if you differ in anything,"** is an all-encompassing saying, and is not limited to only those few matters that happen to agree with the ever-changing beliefs of the secularist-humanists. Furthermore, the statement **"if indeed you believe in Allaah and the Last Day"** clearly makes mankind's referring all matters back to their Lord a condition of faith for anyone who makes the claim to believe in God and the Last Day. For anyone who says that they believe in God and that they will meet Him when they die, and then refuses to believe that this same Creator actually sent down revelation and absolute guidance to His creation, is not being truthful in his or her claim to faith.

No matter how skilled modern day secularist-humanists might be in dealing with many worldly affairs, they fail to realize that no matter how much knowledge they have acquired, that all of it has been facilitated by Allaah. Furthermore, they also fail to realize that their scope of understanding is still terrifically limited, and that in reality, they do not know or understand where mankind is headed, and what is best for them in this life or the next. For this reason, it would not make sense to blindly follow the trends they set and reject the way of an All-Wise, All-Knowing Creator.

﴿ ثُمَّ جَعَلْنَٰكَ عَلَىٰ شَرِيعَةٍ مِّنَ ٱلْأَمْرِ فَٱتَّبِعْهَا وَلَا تَتَّبِعْ أَهْوَآءَ ٱلَّذِينَ لَا يَعْلَمُونَ ﴿١٨﴾ ﴾

Then We put you, (O Muhammad), **on a plain way of (Our) commandment. So follow you that way, and follow not the desires of those who know not.**
[45:18]

The religious affairs that Muslims are being pressured to abandon are the same things that do not happen to agree with the ever-changing values of liberalism, humanism and secularism. However, the fact that something is not liked by a people is not a proof of its incorrectness, as it is known that there are many things in our lives which we might not incline towards at first, but we know are essential for our survival and well-being.

﴿ وَعَسَىٰٓ أَن تَكْرَهُوا۟ شَيْـًٔا وَهُوَ خَيْرٌ لَّكُمْ ۖ وَعَسَىٰٓ أَن تُحِبُّوا۟ شَيْـًٔا وَهُوَ شَرٌّ لَّكُمْ ۗ وَٱللَّهُ يَعْلَمُ وَأَنتُمْ لَا تَعْلَمُونَ ﴾

It may be that you dislike a thing which is good for you, and that you like a thing which is bad for you. And Allaah knows, while you do not know.
[2:216]

Interestingly, people are willing to be patient about getting up early in the morning to go to work, taking medicine that might have dangerous side effects, and paying fines for driving infractions. However, if their Creator ordains for them that they should wake up early to pray, avoid certain beliefs and acts so they might not harm themselves and others, or give a small portion of their earnings away in alms tax, many people begin to reject these matters.

Consequently, it can be understood that the likes and dislikes of a people cannot be used as a yardstick in understanding right and wrong, especially when dealing with those who are fickle and limited by nature.

Altering God's Religion According to Desire

In his *New York Times* column, Rushdie calls upon the Muslims to hasten to alter their religion in order to "modernize." Rushdie states that the restoration of religion "to the sphere of the personal, its depoliticization, is the nettle that all Muslim societies must grasp in order to become modern." However, Rushdie has erred when he attributes this kind of baseless altering of Allaah's religion to being a sign of modernization. On the contrary, this approach to understanding religion existed in the time of the prophets, as can be found in the *Qur'aan* which was revealed over 1,400 years ago:

﴿ وَإِذَا تُتْلَىٰ عَلَيْهِمْ ءَايَاتُنَا بَيِّنَـٰتٍ قَالَ ٱلَّذِينَ لَا يَرْجُونَ لِقَآءَنَا ٱئْتِ بِقُرْءَانٍ غَيْرِ هَـٰذَآ أَوْ بَدِّلْهُ ۚ قُلْ مَا يَكُونُ لِىٓ أَنْ أُبَدِّلَهُۥ مِن تِلْقَآئِ نَفْسِىٓ ۖ إِنْ أَتَّبِعُ إِلَّا مَا يُوحَىٰٓ إِلَىَّ ۖ إِنِّىٓ أَخَافُ إِنْ عَصَيْتُ رَبِّى عَذَابَ يَوْمٍ عَظِيمٍ ۝١٥ ﴾

And when Our Clear Verses are recited unto them, those who hope not for their meeting with Us, say: "Bring us a *Qur'aan* other than this, or change it." Say (to them): "It is not for me to change it on my own accord; I only follow that which is revealed unto me. Verily, I fear the torment of the Great Day [the Day of Resurrection] **if I were to disobey my Lord."**
[10:15]

Salman Rushdie is either unaware, forgets, or purposely overlooks the fact that Allaah addressed the polytheists in the time of the Prophet (ﷺ), asking them:

﴿ أَلَمۡ تَعۡلَمۡ أَنَّ ٱللَّهَ لَهُۥ مُلۡكُ ٱلسَّمَٰوَٰتِ وَٱلۡأَرۡضِ ﴾

"Know you not that to Allaah (alone) belongs the dominion of the heavens and the earth?"
[5:40]

Since everything that Allaah created in the heavens and the earth belongs to Him alone, is He not the one who also possesses the right to command the affairs within this creation? Does He have any partners who share in His absolute ownership of the universe, who would then possess the right to command His creation as they please?

﴿ أَلَا لَهُ ٱلۡخَلۡقُ وَٱلۡأَمۡرُ ﴾

Surely, His is the Creation <u>and</u> the Commandment.
[7:54]

One wonders if Rushdie has any logical proof to show his readers that the Creator's command is only limited to creational matters such as creating, sustaining and administering the affairs of the universe. Does any kind of logical proof exist to substantiate how the Creator does not also possess the right to command within legislative matters, such as the establishment of a religion and way of life that is acceptable to Him? In short, Rushdie is requested to consider how he forms his incoherent distinction of differentiating between Allaah's **creational** and **legislative**[87] command. Why believe in one, but not the other?

﴿ قُلۡ إِنَّ ٱلۡأَمۡرَ كُلَّهُۥ لِلَّهِ ﴾

Say (to them): "Indeed the Command belongs wholly to Allaah."
[3:154]

Rushdie sees this move to the sphere of indefiniteness as being a form of progression, whereas he sees a move to apply the Creator's religion in anything more than a nominal way as being a form of regression. Relegating

[87] Muhammad ibn Saalih al-'Uthaymeen, *Sharh Thalaathatul-Usool*, p.85, *Daar ath-Thuriyyaa lin-Nashr.*

Allaah's command "to the sphere of the personal" requires picking and choosing things from Allaah's commandments according to personal likes and dislikes alone. Either the entire religion is from Allaah and should be accepted as a whole, or it is from other than Him, and can be rejected in whole or in part.

﴿ أَفَتُؤْمِنُونَ بِبَعْضِ ٱلْكِتَـٰبِ وَتَكْفُرُونَ بِبَعْضٍ ۚ فَمَا جَزَآءُ مَن يَفْعَلُ ذَٰلِكَ مِنكُمْ إِلَّا خِزْىٌ فِى ٱلْحَيَوٰةِ ٱلدُّنْيَا ۖ وَيَوْمَ ٱلْقِيَـٰمَةِ يُرَدُّونَ إِلَىٰٓ أَشَدِّ ٱلْعَذَابِ ۗ وَمَا ٱللَّهُ بِغَـٰفِلٍ عَمَّا تَعْمَلُونَ ﴾

Do you believe in a part of the Scripture and disbelieve in the rest? For what is the recompense of those who do so among you, except disgrace in the life of this world; and on the Day of Resurrection they shall be consigned to the most grievous torment. And Allaah is not unaware of what you do.
[2:85]

The True Reality Behind Secularist Thought

Rushdie's secularist way of thinking maintains that religion should be for God, meaning; things that are limited to rites and acts of worship belong to Him, whereas mankind's social and political destiny should be left in the hands of mankind, as if they know better. One of the problems with this ideology is that those who believe that religion should be for God and the State should be for the people, in actuality, often do not even allow God to interfere in their religious rites and acts of worship as they claim. Even in the limited sphere they have set aside for God - being that of religious rites and acts of worship - these people take it upon themselves to formulate a religion[88] that they can follow. In reality, they do not even recognize Allaah's authority to ordain a religion for them, even if it solely consisted of rites and acts of worship. In formulating their own religions, they take themselves to be partners with Allaah in His right to legislate a religion and way of life for the creation.

[88] "What Americans are saying is, 'Listen, I can probably put together a philosophy of life for myself that is just as accurate, just as helpful as any particular faith might provide.'" (Quote from David Kinnaman. See: K. Connie Kang, Most believe in heaven and think they'll go there, *Los Angeles Times*, October 25, 2003.)

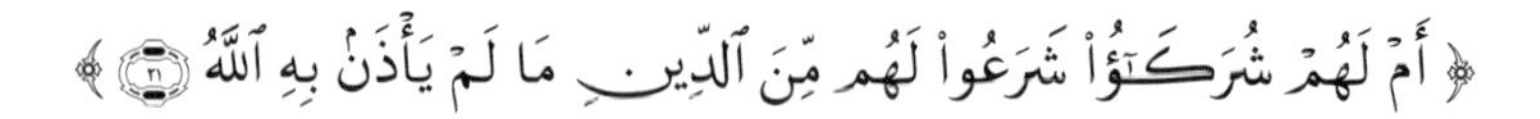

“Or do they have partners that legislate a religion for them which Allaah has not given any permission for?”
[42:21]

In an article entitled “Church backs raves to bring in young people,” *The Telegraph*’s Jonathan Petre reported that the Church of England “gave its official blessing to alternative forms of youth worship such as ‘raves in the nave’ yesterday as part of its efforts to attract young people into church.”

The General Synod sanctioned their national youth strategy by encouraging raves, hoping that this would be a means of attracting youth back to the Church. However, this did not occur without incident. Petre notes that the most notorious of episodes was the “nine o’clock service” in Sheffield, which he notes, “was closed down after allegations of improper relations between the clergyman and female members of the congregation.”[89]

One wonders how the Anglican Church presumes they possess the right to devise these “alternative forms of youth worship,” as if the Creator Himself does not know how He wills to be worshipped:

﴿أَمۡ لَكُمۡ سُلۡطَٰنٞ مُّبِينٞ ١٥٦ فَأۡتُواْ بِكِتَٰبِكُمۡ إِن كُنتُمۡ صَٰدِقِينَ ١٥٧﴾

Or have you a manifest authority (from Allaah)? Then bring your Book, if you are truthful.
[37:156-157]

These types of unauthorized acts of worship have had their precedent set by earlier Christians. For example, the Romans merged the practice of their pagan religion’s celebration of the sun god into the religion which the Prophet Jesus (عليه السلام) had been sent with. To this day, Christians celebrate this festival, believing that Jesus (عليه السلام) was born on the 25th of December. This is so, even though there is nothing in the Bible that corroborates such a thing. It is in fact the day of celebration for Mithras, the Roman sun god,

[89] Jonathan Petre, Church backs raves to bring in young people, *The Telegraph*, November 16, 2002.

whose festival of the solstice had traditionally been celebrated on the 25th of December.[90]

In short, most of those who adhere to secularism claim that they at least recognize God's right to legislate or decide in affairs that are limited to rites of worship. This is what they say when they claim that the State should be for the people, and religion for God. However, a closer examination of their beliefs and actions shows that they often do not even recognize God's right to decide in the most basic acts of worship. In the end, they actually end up believing that the State should be for the people, as well as religion too.

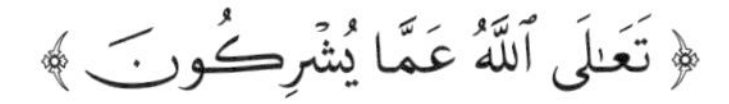

High and Exalted is Allaah above all that they associate as partners (with Him).
[27:63]

A Glaring Lack of Trust and Certainty

Many people trust that their Creator's comprehensive knowledge, wisdom and justice brings about order in the creation of the universe. Had there been partners with Him in the affairs of creation, surely, everything contained within the universe would be in a state of chaos and confusion. This disorder would occur, as it would be impossible for a group of creators to agree upon everything. If there had been many gods, each god would have taken away what the other created, and some would have tried to overcome others. Under these circumstances, complete chaos would result in the creation and administration of the universe.

﴿ لَوْ كَانَ فِيهِمَآ ءَالِهَةٌ إِلَّا ٱللَّهُ لَفَسَدَتَا ۚ فَسُبْحَـٰنَ ٱللَّهِ رَبِّ ٱلْعَرْشِ عَمَّا يَصِفُونَ ﴾

Had there been in the heavens and the earth gods besides Allaah, both would indeed have been ruined. Glorified is Allaah, the Lord of the Throne; (High is He) above all that they associate with Him.
[21:21-22]

---

[90] *Collier's Encyclopedia* (New York: Macmillan Educational Company, 1990), Volume 6, p.403.

Instead of witnessing disorder within the universe, we witness a breathtakingly ordered system, which is a proof of the unity of the Creator and the absence of partners who create alongside Him.

﴿ ٱلَّذِى خَلَقَ سَبۡعَ سَمَٰوَٰتٍ طِبَاقًاۖ مَّا تَرَىٰ فِى خَلۡقِ ٱلرَّحۡمَٰنِ مِن تَفَٰوُتٍۖ فَٱرۡجِعِ ٱلۡبَصَرَ هَلۡ تَرَىٰ مِن فُطُورٍ ۝٣ ثُمَّ ٱرۡجِعِ ٱلۡبَصَرَ كَرَّتَيۡنِ يَنقَلِبۡ إِلَيۡكَ ٱلۡبَصَرُ خَاسِئًا وَهُوَ حَسِيرٌ ۝٤ ﴾

(He) Who has created the seven heavens one above another; you can see no fault in the creation of the Most Merciful. Then look again: Can you see any rifts? Then look again and yet again: your sight will return to you humbled, in a state of fatigue.
[67:3-4]

Those who affirm the existence of a Creator do not normally question His capability in creating and administrating the affairs of the universe. Had there been multiple creators and sustainers, the whole universe would be in a state of chaos. Likewise, if people set up partners with Allaah in His legislating a religion and way of life for them, in the end, they will only bring chaos, confusion and eventual ruin upon themselves and their societies.

The Consequences of Following Incorrect Beliefs and False Ideologies

A Creation Brought Into Existence Without Knowledge, Will and Ability?

It has already preceded in this work that a portion of mankind denies the existence of a Creator, believing that they have been brought into existence solely by feats of nature. Shaykh as-Sa'dee notes that according to these people, "this nature does not have any sense of consciousness in what occurs from it of feats. Instead, it is but a mere mechanism. In spite of this, there emanates from this nature great exploits that are at the peak of origination and proficiency, and the utmost degree of wisdom and mercy, and with the highest level of union upon which all matters become upright, and all situations are rectified. (All of this apparently occurs) without a planner, creator or initiator."[91]

This proficiency, wisdom and mercy can be witnessed within the creation of our own selves, notes Shaykh 'Abdur-Razzaaq al-'Abbaad: "Consider the beginning, middle and end of your creation. Look with all insight at the beginning of your creation, from a trickle of insignificant fluid; whereby the Lord of all lords extracted this fluid from between the backbone and ribs, guided it by His Might with the narrowness of its channels and the diversity of its passages, up until (the point that) He brings it to its abode and place of assembly.

See how Allaah united the male and female and placed love between them, and how He led them with the chain of desire and love to come together, which is the cause behind the synthesis and formation of a child.

Look at how He predestined the meeting of those two fluids despite the distance between each of them. He brought the two fluids from the

---

[91] Shaykh 'Abdur-Rahmaan as-Sa'dee, *al-Adillatul-Qawaati' wal-Baraaheen fee Ibtaal Usool-il-Mulhideen*, *Daarul-Minhaaj*, p.28.

depth of veins and organs and gathered them to one place. He prescribed for them a firmly established dwelling. Air cannot get to it to spoil it; cold cannot get to it to harden or congeal it, and no obstacle can reach it.

He then transforms that white saturated trickle into a dark red clinging entity, then He makes it into a chewed lump (of flesh), completely different to the clinging body in its colour, essence and form. Allaah then fashions it into bare bones, distinct from the chewed lump in form, look, proportion, feel, and colour. In this manner, the stages of a person's creation gradually progress until he emerges in these forms that Allaah has fashioned him with; He originated for him, hearing, sight, a mouth, a nose, and the rest of the openings. He extended and expanded his legs and arms, separated their ends into fingers and toes, and then further split them into phalanxes. He also assembled the inner organs such as the heart, stomach, liver, spleen, lungs, womb, vesica and intestines; each one having a proportion and benefit specific to it. So how perfect is the One who created, proportioned, measured and guided (each thing appropriately)."[92]

﴿ وَهُوَ ٱلَّذِىٓ أَنشَأَ لَكُمُ ٱلسَّمْعَ وَٱلْأَبْصَـٰرَ وَٱلْأَفْـِٔدَةَ ۚ قَلِيلًا مَّا تَشْكُرُونَ ٧٨ ﴾

It is He Who has created for you hearing, sight, and hearts (understanding). Little is the thanks you give.
[23:78]

As-Sa'dee asks those who adopt these atheistic beliefs the following questions: "'Who is it that originated these countless and magnificent forms of creation? And who is it that consolidated this splendid precision within the creation? And who is it that ordered the creation's astonishing movements that bewilder us when considering their beauty and perfection of arrangement?'

They will answer: 'Indeed, all of these affairs come about by chance and feats of blind nature which do not possess **knowledge**, **will** and **ability**, or any other kind of attribute!'"

As-Sa'dee answers these types of doubts in the following way: "Were you to abandon these great worlds to chance and chaos for an hour -

[92] Shaykh 'Abdur-Razzaaq al-'Abbaad, *Asbaab Ziyaadatil-Eemaan wa Nuqsaanihi, Ghiraas lin-Nashr wat-Tawzi'*, pp.42-43.

rather, for an instant - the heavens and the earth would cease to exist and the worlds would become completely disordered:"[93]

﴿ ۞ إِنَّ ٱللَّهَ يُمۡسِكُ ٱلسَّمَٰوَٰتِ وَٱلۡأَرۡضَ أَن تَزُولَاۚ وَلَئِن زَالَتَآ إِنۡ أَمۡسَكَهُمَا مِنۡ أَحَدٖ مِّنۢ بَعۡدِهِۦٓۚ إِنَّهُۥ كَانَ حَلِيمًا غَفُورٗا ٤١ ﴾

Verily, Allaah grasps the heavens and the earth lest they should move away from their places; and if they were to move away from their places, there is none that could grasp them after Him. Truly, He is Most Forbearing, Oft-Forgiving.
[35:41]

The Doubts of the Polytheists

Another portion of mankind affirms the existence of a Creator, however, they deem it permissible to worship Him along with others from amongst the creation. Most often, they do not believe that these created things they worship have any share with the Creator in creating, sustaining, and administrating the affairs of the universe. However, they usually claim that they only worship these created beings and things as intercessors, to bring them closer to the Creator:

﴿ وَيَعۡبُدُونَ مِن دُونِ ٱللَّهِ مَا لَا يَضُرُّهُمۡ وَلَا يَنفَعُهُمۡ وَيَقُولُونَ هَٰٓؤُلَآءِ شُفَعَٰٓؤُنَا عِندَ ٱللَّهِۚ قُلۡ أَتُنَبِّـُٔونَ ٱللَّهَ بِمَا لَا يَعۡلَمُ فِي ٱلسَّمَٰوَٰتِ وَلَا فِي ٱلۡأَرۡضِۚ سُبۡحَٰنَهُۥ وَتَعَٰلَىٰ عَمَّا يُشۡرِكُونَ ١٨ ﴾

"And they worship besides Allaah, things that do not harm them, nor benefit them, while they say, "These are our intercessors with Allaah." Say (to them), "Do you inform Allaah about that which He knows not in the heavens and the earth?" Glorified and Exalted is He above all which they associate as partners with Him."
[10:18]

[93] Shaykh 'Abdur-Rahmaan as-Sa'dee, *al-Adillatul-Qawaati' wal-Baraaheen fee Ibtaal Usool-il-Mulhideen*, *Daarul-Minhaaj*, p.41.

If you were to stop one of these individuals and ask them who created, sustains, possesses and controls everything within the universe without exception, they will certainly say "God." This confession is the greatest proof they could possibly bring against themselves, as demonstrated in the following verse of the *Qur'aan*:

﴿ قُل لِّمَنِ ٱلۡأَرۡضُ وَمَن فِيهَآ إِن كُنتُمۡ تَعۡلَمُونَ ٨٤ سَيَقُولُونَ لِلَّهِۚ قُلۡ أَفَلَا تَذَكَّرُونَ ٨٥ قُلۡ مَن رَّبُّ ٱلسَّمَٰوَٰتِ ٱلسَّبۡعِ وَرَبُّ ٱلۡعَرۡشِ ٱلۡعَظِيمِ ٨٦ سَيَقُولُونَ لِلَّهِۚ قُلۡ أَفَلَا تَتَّقُونَ ٨٧ قُلۡ مَنۢ بِيَدِهِۦ مَلَكُوتُ كُلِّ شَيۡءٖ وَهُوَ يُجِيرُ وَلَا يُجَارُ عَلَيۡهِ إِن كُنتُمۡ تَعۡلَمُونَ ٨٨ سَيَقُولُونَ لِلَّهِۚ قُلۡ فَأَنَّىٰ تُسۡحَرُونَ ٨٩ بَلۡ أَتَيۡنَٰهُم بِٱلۡحَقِّ وَإِنَّهُمۡ لَكَٰذِبُونَ ٩٠ ﴾

Say (to them): "To whom belongs the earth and all beings therein, if you know?" They will say, "To Allaah." Say: "Will you not then remember?"

Say: "Who is (the) Lord of the seven heavens, and (the) Lord of the Great Throne?"

They will say: "Allaah." Say: "Will you not then fear Him?"

Say: "In Whose Hand is the sovereignty and treasures of everything? And He protects (all), while against whom there is no protector,[94] if you know?" They will say: "(All that belongs) to Allaah." Say: "How then are you deluded away from the truth?"

Nay, We have brought them the truth, and verily, they are liars.
[23:84-90]

[94] Meaning: If Allaah saves anyone, none can punish or harm them, and if Allaah punishes or harms anyone, none can save them.

The Source of All Liberalist Ideologies

Another portion of humankind affirms the existence of the Creator, yet believes that this All-Wise, All-Knowing Creator did not send down any guidance to His creation as to how they should live and worship Him. Similar to this group, another portion of mankind affirms the existence of the Creator as well as the existence of books that have been sent down to mankind by way of chosen messengers. However, despite their awareness of these prophets, they have no firm belief that the Creator intended for them to live by one chosen way. Instead, both these groups of people live by the principle that there is no one particular way to God, and that it is up to each individual to choose their own way.

After denying that the Creator has chosen and legislated one way for mankind, these aforementioned groups band together and begin to formulate man-made ideologies. According to pollster David Kinnaman, it is their belief that mankind can invent a religion and way of life that is "just as accurate, just as helpful as any particular faith might provide.'"[95]

Because people believe in something that Kinnaman refers to as "hyper-individualism," they believe that it is correct to "mix secular and various religious views to create their personal belief systems." Because these people "don't mind embracing contradictions," they are "cutting and pasting religious views from a variety of different sources - television, movies, [and] conversations with their friends."[96]

﴿ وَمَنْ أَضَلُّ مِمَّنِ ٱتَّبَعَ هَوَىٰهُ بِغَيْرِ هُدًى مِّنَ ٱللَّهِ ۚ
إِنَّ ٱللَّهَ لَا يَهْدِى ٱلْقَوْمَ ٱلظَّٰلِمِينَ ﴾

And who is more astray than one who follows his own desire without guidance from Allaah? Verily Allaah guides not a wrong doing people.
[28:50]

Once people rely on the opinions of the ever-changing conjecture of human thought, they set about inventing different ideologies they feel will

---

[95] K. Connie Kang, Most believe in heaven and think they'll go there, *Los Angeles Times*, October 25, 2003.

[96] Ibid.

serve them well. **This ever-changing conjecture is the source of all man-made ideologies**, such as atheism, agnosticism, existentialism, humanism, liberalism, democracy, pluralism, secularism, Marxism, communism, and many others.

All of these materialist ideologies are based upon the belief that God does not exist, or that He exists, but failed to reveal a complete message to His creation. Some people believe that His revelation is only relevant for ancient times, as if the Creator did not know how things would be in this time. Others believe that we have been given the freedom to accept or reject what we want from His revelation, as if people are more knowledgeable than Him as to what benefits them. One wonders, therefore, if it is truly befitting to place such skepticism upon the One who created everything that exists.

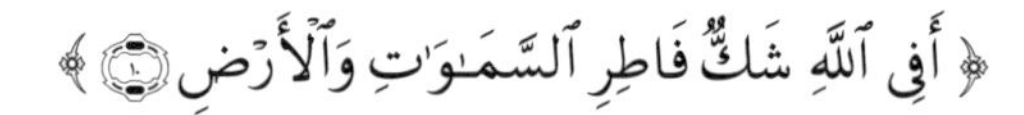

Is there doubt about Allaah, Creator of the heavens and the earth?
[14:10]

Regarding these types of doubts, as-Sa'dee stated: "It is not befitting of Allaah's Mercy, Wisdom and Praiseworthiness, that He leave His servants futilely neglected, without a message, and (without) something which acquaints them with that which will order and amend their worldly and religious condition. Therefore, He sent the messengers and sent down the books, out of His Wisdom and Mercy; so that there may not be a proof for the people against Allaah after the sending of the messengers, that they may say: "No bringer of good tidings or warner ever came to us."[97]

Because those who profess these man-made ideologies possess neither textual nor logical evidences to back up what they believe in, they continue to search for new theories that will repeatedly prove that what they were deeming to be correct today will turn out to have been incorrect within a short period of time. Once this is understood, would it seem reasonable to favour these ever-changing theories over the clear proofs and evidences that exist in the Creator's revelation?

[97] Shaykh 'Abdur-Rahmaan as-Sa'dee, *al-Adillatul-Qawaati' wal-Baraaheen fee Ibtaal Usool-il-Mulhideen*, *Daarul-Minhaaj*, p.10.

﴿ فَبِأَيِّ حَدِيثٍ بَعْدَ ٱللَّهِ وَءَايَٰتِهِۦ يُؤْمِنُونَ ﴾

Then in which speech after Allaah and His verses will they believe?
[45:6]

The Danger of Blindly Following Others

The Creator has forbidden His creation from following all these different forms of conjecture, their initiators, and their followers, even if they be great in number:

﴿ وَلَا تُطِعْ مَنْ أَغْفَلْنَا قَلْبَهُۥ عَن ذِكْرِنَا وَٱتَّبَعَ هَوَىٰهُ وَكَانَ أَمْرُهُۥ فُرُطًا ﴾

And do not obey him whose heart We have made heedless of Our Remembrance, and who follows his own desire, and whose affair [deeds] **has been lost.**
[18:28]

Anyone who prefers these contradictory, ever-changing ways over the chosen Way of the Creator, has shown that they do not truly believe in the Creator and the guidance He sent down to mankind. Instead, they disbelieve in it as a whole, or only believe in those aspects of His message that agree with the conjecture of their chosen theorists, rejecting the rest.

﴿ وَمَنْ أَظْلَمُ مِمَّنِ ٱفْتَرَىٰ عَلَى ٱللَّهِ كَذِبًا أَوْ كَذَّبَ بِٱلْحَقِّ لَمَّا جَآءَهُۥٓ ﴾

And who does more wrong than he who invents a lie against Allaah, or denies the truth when it comes to him?
[29:68]

An Unsubstantiated Doubt Surrounding the Coming of The Day of Judgement

For every action a person chooses to take in his or her life, consequences must necessarily arise from the choices they make. This is especially so for our eventual resurrection and judgement in the hereafter. Indeed, the eventual occurrence of the Day of Judgement is a principle aspect of belief according to the revealed scriptures. Contrary to this, a portion of mankind disbelieves in the coming of the Last Hour, as has been mentioned in the *Qur'aan*:

﴿ وَقَالُوٓاْ إِنْ هِىَ إِلَّا حَيَاتُنَا ٱلدُّنْيَا وَمَا نَحْنُ بِمَبْعُوثِينَ ﴿٢٩﴾ ﴾

And they said: "There is no (other life) but our (present) life of this world, and never shall we be resurrected."
[6:29]

Interestingly, those who deny the Day of Judgement often also affirm the existence of a Creator. Once they affirm that a Creator exists who created them from nothing, it would not be possible for them to explain how the Creator cannot refashion that which He originated before. This materialist way of thinking is not something new. On the contrary, Allaah refutes this claim in the *Qur'aan*, clarifying that doubting His ability to recreate something He has already created involves comparing His ability with that of the creation:

﴿ وَضَرَبَ لَنَا مَثَلًا وَنَسِىَ خَلْقَهُۥ ۖ قَالَ مَن يُحْىِ ٱلْعِظَـٰمَ وَهِىَ رَمِيمٌ ﴿٧٨﴾
قُلْ يُحْيِيهَا ٱلَّذِىٓ أَنشَأَهَآ أَوَّلَ مَرَّةٍ ۖ وَهُوَ بِكُلِّ خَلْقٍ عَلِيمٌ ﴿٧٩﴾ ﴾

And he puts forth a comparison for Us and forgets his own creation, saying: "Who will give life to these bones after they are rotted and have become dust?"

Say (to them):"He will give life to them Who created them for the first time. And He is the All-Knower of every creation."
[36:78-79]

These verses show that one who doubts Allaah's capability to recreate something has actually forgotten about his or her own origins. Was that person not a nonentity before finding him or herself present in this world? If that is the case, why would it be difficult for this Creator to refashion what He had already made before?

Furthermore, when somebody reflects upon the greatness of what is contained within the heavens and the earth, surely, this must lead them to realize that these aspects of creation are much greater in nature than their own creation. Consequently, there is no legitimate reason to believe in the existence of a Creator, yet doubt that this same All-Knowing Creator does not have full knowledge of, or cannot reassemble what is contained within the graves.[98]

[98] Shaykh 'Abdur-Rahmaan as-Sa'dee, *Tayseer al-Kareem ar-Rahmaan fee Tafseer Kalaam al-Mannaan*, *Mu'asasah ar-Risaalah*, pp.699-700.

In short, once one has accepted that Allaah exists, this belief necessitates that this Creator would recompense His servants for their deeds; either good with good, or bad with bad. States as-Sa'dee: "And He has indeed informed (His servants) in more than one place (of the *Qur'aan*) that He, glorified is He (above what they attribute to Him), did not create the world in vain; rather, **(He created them) for the recompense.**"[99]

﴿وَأَنذِرْهُمْ يَوْمَ ٱلْحَسْرَةِ إِذْ قُضِىَ ٱلْأَمْرُ وَهُمْ فِى غَفْلَةٍ وَهُمْ لَا يُؤْمِنُونَ ﴿٣٩﴾﴾

And warn them (O Muhammad) **of the Day of grief and regrets, when the case will be decided, while (now) they are in a state of heedlessness, and they believe not.**
[19:39]

The Arrival of This Day

Most people eagerly read the newspapers every day in order to find out what is occurring in the world today. Although there is nothing wrong with wanting to know what is going on in the world, it is certainly a strange matter to consider that many people are not concerned about the news of what will occur to them when they die, are buried, and raised up for judgement on the Day of Reckoning.

The One who knows all that has happened and all that will happen, describes the Day of Resurrection in the *Qur'aan* in a detailed manner:

﴿يَسْـَٔلُونَكَ عَنِ ٱلسَّاعَةِ أَيَّانَ مُرْسَىٰهَا ۖ قُلْ إِنَّمَا عِلْمُهَا عِندَ رَبِّى ۖ لَا يُجَلِّيهَا لِوَقْتِهَآ إِلَّا هُوَ ۚ ثَقُلَتْ فِى ٱلسَّمَٰوَٰتِ وَٱلْأَرْضِ ۚ لَا تَأْتِيكُمْ إِلَّا بَغْتَةً ۗ ﴿١٨٧﴾﴾

They ask you about the Hour (Day of Resurrection)**: "When will be its appointed time?" Say (to them): "The knowledge thereof is with my Lord (alone). None can reveal its time but He. Heavy is its burden through the heavens and the earth. It shall not come upon you except all of a sudden."**
[7:187]

---

[99] Shaykh 'Abdur-Rahmaan as-Sa'dee, op. cit., p.24.

The Day of Judgement is described in the *Qur'aan* as being a day in which the present creation will be altered:

﴿ فَإِذَا نُفِخَ فِي ٱلصُّورِ نَفۡخَةٞ وَٰحِدَةٞ ١٣ وَحُمِلَتِ ٱلۡأَرۡضُ وَٱلۡجِبَالُ فَدُكَّتَا دَكَّةٗ وَٰحِدَةٗ ١٤ ﴾

Then when the Trumpet will be blown with one blowing [the first one]**. And the earth and the mountains shall be removed from their places, and crushed with a single crushing.**
[69:13-14]

It is described that the sky will be cleft asunder, the stars will scatter, the seas will burst forth and the earth will be pounded to powder. Then a level plain will be made, from which humankind will be raised:

﴿ وَتَرَى ٱلۡأَرۡضَ بَارِزَةٗ وَحَشَرۡنَٰهُمۡ فَلَمۡ نُغَادِرۡ مِنۡهُمۡ أَحَدٗا ٤٧ ﴾

And you will see the earth as a level plain, and We shall gather them altogether, so as not to leave one of them behind.
[18:47]

The time that the prophets were commanded to warn about will have come:

﴿ إِن كَانَتۡ إِلَّا صَيۡحَةٗ وَٰحِدَةٗ فَإِذَا هُمۡ جَمِيعٞ لَّدَيۡنَا مُحۡضَرُونَ ٥٣ ﴾

It will be but a single blast, so behold they will all be brought up before Us.
[36:53]

The souls shall be joined with the bodies, and humankind will be raised from the ground, barefoot, naked and uncircumcised, as they had been created the first time. The people will be raised in a state of bewilderment:

﴿ قَالُواْ يَٰوَيۡلَنَا مَنۢ بَعَثَنَا مِن مَّرۡقَدِنَاۜۗ هَٰذَا مَا وَعَدَ ٱلرَّحۡمَٰنُ وَصَدَقَ ٱلۡمُرۡسَلُونَ ٥٢ ﴾

They will say: "Woe to us! Who has raised us up from our place of sleep?" (It will be said to them): "This is what the Most Gracious (Allaah) had promised, and the Messengers spoke the truth."
[36:52]

All of humankind ever created will be raised on that same level plain in an unprecedented assembly, feeling that they had only lived on the earth for a day, or part of a day. Relatives will be made to see each other, and no person shall have the ability or will to do anything for another. Such will be the fear that shall be felt.

﴿ وَلَوْ تَرَىٰٓ إِذْ وُقِفُوا۟ عَلَىٰ رَبِّهِمْ ۚ قَالَ أَلَيْسَ هَـٰذَا بِٱلْحَقِّ ۚ ﴿٣٠﴾ ﴾

If you could but see when they will be brought and made to stand in front of their Lord. He will say: "Is this [the Resurrection and the Reckoning] **not the Truth?"**
[6:30]

This is the Day that every word spoken, every action taken and every belief that was accepted will be brought forward, even if it were an atom's weight of good or evil. Sectarian differences will be judged according to the criterion that existed in the Creator's revelation. Those who oppressed others will be taken to account.

﴿ فَٱلْيَوْمَ لَا تُظْلَمُ نَفْسٌ شَيْـًٔا وَلَا تُجْزَوْنَ إِلَّا مَا كُنتُمْ تَعْمَلُونَ ﴿٥٤﴾ ﴾

This Day, no soul will be wronged in a single thing, nor will you be rewarded except for what you used to do.
[36:54]

The Final Outcome

A party will be in Heaven, whilst another party will be in Hell. This will be the end result of the beliefs and actions we choose for ourselves while living in this short life.

﴿ ۞ قُلْ يَـٰعِبَادِىَ ٱلَّذِينَ أَسْرَفُوا۟ عَلَىٰٓ أَنفُسِهِمْ لَا تَقْنَطُوا۟ مِن رَّحْمَةِ ٱللَّهِ ۚ إِنَّ ٱللَّهَ يَغْفِرُ ٱلذُّنُوبَ جَمِيعًا ۚ إِنَّهُۥ هُوَ ٱلْغَفُورُ ٱلرَّحِيمُ ﴿٥٣﴾ وَأَنِيبُوٓا۟ إِلَىٰ رَبِّكُمْ وَأَسْلِمُوا۟ لَهُۥ مِن قَبْلِ

أَن يَأْتِيَكُمُ ٱلْعَذَابُ ثُمَّ لَا تُنصَرُونَ ﴿٥٤﴾ وَٱتَّبِعُوٓا۟ أَحْسَنَ مَآ أُنزِلَ إِلَيْكُم مِّن
رَّبِّكُم مِّن قَبْلِ أَن يَأْتِيَكُمُ ٱلْعَذَابُ بَغْتَةً وَأَنتُمْ لَا تَشْعُرُونَ ﴿٥٥﴾ أَن تَقُولَ
نَفْسٌ يَٰحَسْرَتَىٰ عَلَىٰ مَا فَرَّطتُ فِى جَنۢبِ ٱللَّهِ وَإِن كُنتُ لَمِنَ ٱلسَّٰخِرِينَ ﴿٥٦﴾ أَوْ تَقُولَ
لَوْ أَنَّ ٱللَّهَ هَدَىٰنِى لَكُنتُ مِنَ ٱلْمُتَّقِينَ ﴿٥٧﴾ أَوْ تَقُولَ حِينَ تَرَى ٱلْعَذَابَ لَوْ
أَنَّ لِى كَرَّةً فَأَكُونَ مِنَ ٱلْمُحْسِنِينَ ﴿٥٨﴾ بَلَىٰ قَدْ جَآءَتْكَ ءَايَٰتِى فَكَذَّبْتَ بِهَا
وَٱسْتَكْبَرْتَ وَكُنتَ مِنَ ٱلْكَٰفِرِينَ ﴿٥٩﴾ وَيَوْمَ ٱلْقِيَٰمَةِ تَرَى ٱلَّذِينَ كَذَبُوا۟ عَلَى ٱللَّهِ
وُجُوهُهُم مُّسْوَدَّةٌ ۚ أَلَيْسَ فِى جَهَنَّمَ مَثْوًى لِّلْمُتَكَبِّرِينَ ﴿٦٠﴾ وَيُنَجِّى ٱللَّهُ ٱلَّذِينَ ٱتَّقَوْا۟
بِمَفَازَتِهِمْ لَا يَمَسُّهُمُ ٱلسُّوٓءُ وَلَا هُمْ يَحْزَنُونَ ﴿٦١﴾

Say (to them): "O My servants who have transgressed against themselves; despair not of the Mercy of Allaah: Verily, Allaah forgives all sins. Truly, He is Oft-Forgiving, Most Merciful.

"And turn in repentance and obedience with true faith to your Lord and submit to Him (in Islaam) before the torment comes upon you, (and) then you will not be helped."

"And follow the best of that which is sent down to you from your Lord, before the torment comes on you suddenly while you perceive not."

Lest a person should say: "Alas, (how great is) my regret that I was undutiful to Allaah and that I was among those who mocked."

Or (lest) he should say: "If only Allaah had guided me, I would have been among the righteous."

Or (lest) he should say when he sees the torment: "If only I had another chance (to return to the world), then I would indeed be among those who do good."

Nay! There came to you My Signs, and you denied them, and were proud, and were among the disbelievers.

And on the Day of Resurrection you will see those who lied against Allaah - their faces will be black. Is there not in Hell an abode for the arrogant?

And Allaah will deliver those who are pious and dutiful to their places of success [Heaven]**. Evil shall touch them not, nor shall they grieve.**
[39:54-61]

﴿ وَسِيقَ ٱلَّذِينَ كَفَرُوٓاْ إِلَىٰ جَهَنَّمَ زُمَرًا ۖ حَتَّىٰٓ إِذَا جَآءُوهَا فُتِحَتْ أَبْوَٰبُهَا وَقَالَ لَهُمْ خَزَنَتُهَآ أَلَمْ يَأْتِكُمْ رُسُلٌ مِّنكُمْ يَتْلُونَ عَلَيْكُمْ ءَايَٰتِ رَبِّكُمْ وَيُنذِرُونَكُمْ لِقَآءَ يَوْمِكُمْ هَٰذَا ۚ قَالُواْ بَلَىٰ وَلَٰكِنْ حَقَّتْ كَلِمَةُ ٱلْعَذَابِ عَلَى ٱلْكَٰفِرِينَ ﴿٧١﴾ قِيلَ ٱدْخُلُوٓاْ أَبْوَٰبَ جَهَنَّمَ خَٰلِدِينَ فِيهَا ۖ فَبِئْسَ مَثْوَى ٱلْمُتَكَبِّرِينَ ﴿٧٢﴾ وَسِيقَ ٱلَّذِينَ ٱتَّقَوْاْ رَبَّهُمْ إِلَى ٱلْجَنَّةِ زُمَرًا ۖ حَتَّىٰٓ إِذَا جَآءُوهَا وَفُتِحَتْ أَبْوَٰبُهَا وَقَالَ لَهُمْ خَزَنَتُهَا سَلَٰمٌ عَلَيْكُمْ طِبْتُمْ فَٱدْخُلُوهَا خَٰلِدِينَ ﴿٧٣﴾ وَقَالُواْ ٱلْحَمْدُ لِلَّهِ ٱلَّذِى صَدَقَنَا وَعْدَهُۥ وَأَوْرَثَنَا ٱلْأَرْضَ نَتَبَوَّأُ مِنَ ٱلْجَنَّةِ حَيْثُ نَشَآءُ ۖ فَنِعْمَ أَجْرُ ٱلْعَٰمِلِينَ ﴿٧٤﴾ وَتَرَى ٱلْمَلَٰٓئِكَةَ حَآفِّينَ مِنْ حَوْلِ ٱلْعَرْشِ يُسَبِّحُونَ بِحَمْدِ رَبِّهِمْ ۖ وَقُضِىَ بَيْنَهُم بِٱلْحَقِّ وَقِيلَ ٱلْحَمْدُ لِلَّهِ رَبِّ ٱلْعَٰلَمِينَ ﴿٧٥﴾ ﴾

And those who disbelieved will be driven to Hell in groups till, when they reach it, its gates will suddenly be opened. And its keepers will say, "Did not the Messengers come to you from yourselves, reciting to you the Verses of your Lord, and warning you of the Meeting of this Day of yours?" They will say: "Yes, but the Word of torment has been justified against the disbelievers."

It will be said (to them)**: "Enter you the gates of Hell, to abide therein. And** (indeed) **what an evil abode of the arrogant."**

And those who kept their duty to their Lord will be led to Paradise in groups, till, when they reach it, its gates will be opened and its keepers will say: "Peace be upon you! You have done well, so enter here to abide therein forever."

And they will say: "All praise be to Allaah Who has fulfilled His
Promise to us and has made us inherit (this) land. We can dwell in
Paradise where we will; how excellent a reward
for those who work (righteousness)!"

And you will see the angels surrounding the Throne from all round,
glorifying the praises of their Lord. And it will be judged
between them in truth. And it will be said,
"All praise be to Allaah, Lord of the Worlds."
[39:71-75]